Colouring the Nation

Colouring the Nation

THE TURKEY RED PRINTED COTTON INDUSTRY
IN SCOTLAND c.1840–1940

Stana Nenadic and Sally Tuckett

Published in 2013 by
NMS Enterprises Limited – Publishing
a division of NMS Enterprises Limited
National Museums Scotland
Chambers Street
Edinburgh EH1 1JF

www.nms.ac.uk

Text © Stana Nenadic and Sally Tuckett 2013

The quotation from Richard Holloway's book, *Leaving Alexandria: A Memoir of Faith and Doubt* (2012), is included with the kind permission of Canongate Books, Edinburgh.

Images © National Museums Scotland 2013 with kind permission of Coats plc, unless otherwise credited.

No part of this publication may be reproduced, stored in a retrieval system or transmitted in any form or by any means, electronic, mechanical, photocopying, recording or otherwise, without the prior written permission of the publisher.

The rights of Stana Nenadic and Sally Tuckett to be identified as the authors of this book have been asserted by them in accordance with the Copyright, Designs and Patents Act 1988.

British Library Cataloguing in Publication Data
A catalogue record of this book is available from the British Library.

ISBN: 978–1–905267–80–4

Publication layout and design by
  NMS Enterprises Limited – Publishing.
Cover design by Mark Blackadder.
Cover image and pages 140, 148: Textile sample of Turkey red dyed and cylinder printed cotton with a pattern of stylised peacock tail feathers in diamond burst formations. From the pattern book known as 'Mr Christie's Book' by John Orr Ewing and Co., *c.*1886. Paper, cotton [National Museums Scotland A.1962.1266.10.7.6582].

Printed and bound in Great Britain by Henry Ling Ltd, Dorchester, Dorset.

For a full listing of NMS Enterprises Limited – Publishing titles and related merchandise, visit:
www.nms.ac.uk/books

Colouring the Nation project online

Discover the beauty of the Turkey red collection through a collaborative project between National Museums Scotland and the School of History, Classics and Archaeology, University of Edinburgh. Search the collection, see textile samples up close and uncover the fascinating history of the Scottish Turkey red dyeing and printing industry at:

http://www.nms.ac.uk/turkey_red/colouring_the_nation.aspx

Colouring the Nation is supported by:

Contents

Acknowledgements vii
About the authors ix
Foreword xi

CHAPTER ONE Turkey red in Scotland 1
    Printed cottons in Scotland 2
    William Stirling & Sons 4
    John Orr Ewing & Co. 9
    Archibald Orr Ewing & Co. 11
    The United Turkey Red Co. Ltd 13
    National Museums Scotland Turkey Red Collection 16

CHAPTER TWO Dyeing and printing 23
    The Turkey red process 25
    Printing methods 30
    The rise of synthetic dyes 37

CHAPTER THREE Design, copyright and exhibition 43
    Textile designers 44
    Copyright and copying 50
    Exhibitions of Turkey red 58

CHAPTER FOUR Styles and patterns 67
    Flowers and leaves 68
    Animals and birds 74
    Figures and objects 82
    Abstract and geometric 91

CHAPTER FIVE International markets 97
    North America 98
    India 104
    East Asia, Africa and Australia 110

CHAPTER SIX Home markets 123
    Clothing and home dressmaking 124
    Furnishings 131
    Quilted garments and quilts 136

Select bibliography 141
Select index of names and organisations 145

Acknowledgements

THE AUTHORS wish to thank the following for their assistance, advice and support in the production of this book, and in the research that lies behind the book.

At National Museums Scotland, David Caldwell, Jane Carmichael and Gordon Rintoul, along with Fiona Anderson, Claire Allan, Pam Babes, Elaine MacIntyre, Neil McLean, Lesley Taylor and Hugh Wallace. We are particularly grateful to Graeme Yule, our photographer, and to Lynne Reilly and Kate Blackadder, our editors.

Elsewhere we are indebted to Dinah Eastop of the National Archives at Kew, Linda Eaton of the Winterthur Foundation in the USA, and Richard Ashworth of the Society of Dyers and Colourists in Bradford. Staff at the University of Glasgow Archives, National Library of Scotland, Manchester County Record Office, National Archives and the University of Edinburgh Library have provided every assistance.

Naomi Tarrant and Liz Arthur, distinguished retired curators of textiles at National Museums Scotland and Glasgow Museums respectively, have been both encouraging and helpful, as has Elizabeth Guest, Sonia Ashmore of the Victoria and Albert Museum, London, Maeve Dixon of West Dunbartonshire Council, Phillip Sykas of Manchester Metropolitan University, Anita Quye of the University of Glasgow and Helen Clifford of the University of Warwick. Georgio Riello of the University of Warwick and the Pasold Fund has given support and advice.

At the University of Edinburgh, we would particularly like to thank the following colleagues: Tom Devine, Louise Jackson, Lesley McLean and Trent Orme.

Our research project and this book have benefited from many contributions from workshop participants, particularly those in the Vale of Leven, who have shared their memories and stories of the Turkey red industry and shown us the surviving objects and photographs that they own – in particular, Eona Aitken and the Rev. E. Houston, and most especially local historian, David Harvie, whose insights and knowledge of the area have been invaluable. Jackie Baillie MSP and Gemma Doyle MP have also given their support.

Finally, we are grateful to our funders, the Royal Society of Edinburgh (and the good offices of Anne Fraser, grants administrator), whose generous research grant of 2011 allowed us to undertake the 'Colouring the Nation' project, which has given rise to a digital catalogue and exhibition of the National Museums Scotland Turkey Red Collection that can be viewed on the Museum's website, and which has facilitated the production of this book.

STANA NENADIC
SALLY TUCKETT

About the authors

STANA NENADIC is Professor of Social and Cultural History at the University of Edinburgh. Her research is on the middle classes, élites and businessmen since *c.*1700, and on the material and visual cultures of the past. Recent publications include *Lairds and Luxury: The Highland Gentry in Eighteenth Century Scotland* (2007) and *Scots in London in the Eighteenth Century* (2010). She was Principal Investigator for the two-year research project, with funding from the Royal Society of Edinburgh, which gave rise to this book. Her new project, with funding from the Leverhulme Trust, is titled 'Artisans and the Craft Economy in Scotland, *c.*1780–1914'.

SALLY TUCKETT is a postdoctoral researcher at the University of Edinburgh. Her doctoral work examined the clothing and textile cultures of eighteenth-century Scotland, exploring the production, dissemination and use of utilitarian and decorative dress. She has published articles on national dress in Scotland and the Scottish textile industry in the nineteenth century, the latter produced while postdoctoral researcher on the 'Colouring the Nation' project.

Foreword

WE at National Museums Scotland are delighted to support the publication of this book. This research project, 'Colouring the Nation', has brought one of our lesser known collections into public view as the collection has been assessed, catalogued, digitised and presented online. Not only that, but it has been set in the context of other collections and their scholarly interpretation as set out in this book.

The project sought to redress the balance in popular understanding of Scotland's industrial past as being dominated by heavy industry, to an almost forgotten past which produced textiles that were colourful and a major export earner. This aim has been richly fulfilled through the energy and application of Stana Nenadic and Sally Tuckett. In addition, they have created a legacy of knowledge for the national collection for which we are extremely grateful.

JANE CARMICHAEL
Director of Collections
NATIONAL MUSEUMS SCOTLAND

48" Length of Scarf   6ngd Java   206

OFF

CHAPTER ONE

Turkey red in Scotland

'TURKEY RED' is a bright red fabric dyeing process, typically used on cotton cloth and yarn and produced in large quantities in the nineteenth century. The dyeing process used natural alizarin, which was extracted from madder root along with mordants of oil and alum to fix the dye to the cloth. Other natural but unpleasant substances, including sheep dung, bullocks' blood and urine, were also used in a complex, secretive and lengthy dyeing process that gave a highly valued colour that did not fade in bright sunlight or with frequent washing. The fabric produced was sold as plain red, but was also printed with elaborate and colourful patterns for many uses in Britain and abroad, including clothing, furnishing fabrics and quilts.

Although produced for centuries in the east (hence the name), it was not until the late eighteenth century that European dyers perfected the Turkey red process. It was brought to Scotland by a French entrepreneur in 1785 and quickly adopted by a number of manufacturers with factories on the banks of the River Clyde and in the Vale of Leven in Dunbartonshire. It was a large industry, employing many thousands in the mid- and later nineteenth century, producing millions of yards of dyed and printed cloth and yarn, which was mainly for export. After the early importance of North America, India was the main destination for Scottish Turkey red cottons.

Though competitive and profitable, the Scottish Turkey red industry faced challenges from Manchester factories, and by the end of the nineteenth century the British industry as a whole was gradually undermined by Asian manufacturers and the development of cheaper synthetic dyes from Germany. In an effort to protect their businesses, three prominent Vale of Leven firms – William Stirling & Sons, John Orr Ewing & Co., and Archibald Orr Ewing & Co., amalgamated to form the United Turkey Red Company Ltd (UTR) in 1898. The UTR continued production until 1960, when their final surviving factory closed, bringing the industry to an end after almost 200 years. The pattern book collection of textile samples and designs that forms the

Opposite page:

Textile sample intended for the Indonesian market (see Fig. 1.11).

National Museums Scotland

basis for the 'Colouring the Nation' research project and exhibition in 2013 was acquired by National Museums Scotland in 1962.

Printed cottons in Scotland

The wide availability of cotton textiles from the eighteenth century transformed popular dress. Washable and colourful, cotton is credited with improving general hygiene and enabling working-class participation in fashionable consumption.[1] Cotton, which is commonly regarded as the 'first global commodity', had found its way from India to Europe from the Middle Ages, but availability was greatly increased in the eighteenth century through the trading activities of the East India Company.[2] Indian embroidered and printed cotton, often termed 'calicoes', with their brightly coloured mainly floral motifs, were used for bedding and curtains, and were also a light and cheaper alternative to heavy brocades and silks for clothing the rich and emerging middle ranks. Not everyone was pleased at this development, however; British woollen and linen manufacturers feared the competition and Daniel Defoe, a social commentator in the early eighteenth century, complained that cotton had 'crept into our houses, our closets, our bed-chambers; curtains, cushions, chairs, and at last beds themselves were nothing but Calicoes or Indian stuffs'.[3]

There were numerous government initiatives in the eighteenth century to restrict printed cotton imports from Asia and encourage British cotton textile production. The initial developments were centred on London, where high quality printing workshops emerged to serve the metropolitan fashion market. These workshops used imported plain cloth from India, which was overprinted with local designs, a practice that also soon developed in Scotland alongside the production of printed linen cloth. Companies like the Pollockshaws Printfield Company, which was founded in Renfrewshire in the early 1740s, was particularly noted for the production of printed handkerchiefs, which were later a mainstay of the Turkey red industry.[4] Several of the Turkey red firms that flourished in the nineteenth century began as calico printers, including Todd, Shortridge & Co., owners of the Levenfield Printworks, which was purchased by John Orr Ewing & Co. in 1860 having produced printed cottons from 1768. Another of the Vale of Leven companies, William Stirling & Sons, had begun in the mid-eighteenth century as dealers in London-printed Indian cottons, producing its own printed cottons from the Dalsholm works near Glasgow from the 1760s before relocating to Dunbartonshire in the 1770s. As one of the leading printfield companies in Scotland, William Stirling & Sons was consulted frequently in the late eighteenth century by the Board of Trustees for Fisheries and Manufactures over the state of the textile industry and such issues as design innovation.[5]

By the end of the eighteenth century, cotton had infiltrated Scottish wardrobes across the social spectrum. The first *Statistical Account of Scotland*, written by parish ministers in the 1790s, provides many reports on the use of cotton in all types of garments from gowns and aprons to breeches and stockings. Not everyone approved, of course, because it seemed to generate a greater preoccupation with fashion among the young and, according to an observation for the parish of Wick in the *New Statistical Account of Scotland* of the 1830s, the increased use of cotton had resulted in a rise in rheumatism among the poor, who were no longer protected by the 'homely warm woollen clothing of olden times'. The revolution in dress that cotton clothing introduced was aided by the growing domestic production of cotton thread and cloth. The first cotton mills for spinning cotton thread in Scotland were introduced by English entrepreneurs in the 1770s and were mostly clustered in the Glasgow hinterland on fast flowing rivers for power. David Dale built the most famous factory complex, New Lanark, on the upper reaches of the Clyde, in 1785 [Fig. 1.1]. Coal-fired steam engines resulted in relocation to urban sites in Glasgow and Paisley and the industry flourished in the first half of the nineteenth century, mostly making plain 'grey' yarn and cloth for processing elsewhere. By the 1860s the Scottish cotton industry employed over 40,000 workers, but this was only a fraction of the almost half a million cotton operatives in Lancashire, and by this stage the industry

Figure 1.1

View of New Lanark, 1820. Established in 1785, David Dale's famous cotton spinning village in the rural hinterland of Glasgow was a model for the later Turkey red industry in the Vale of Leven. A print from a contemporary engraving, unknown artist.

Reproduced by permission of the National Library of Scotland was starting to decline due to overseas competition.[6] The sector that was best able to survive in Scotland was cotton dyeing and printing, including Turkey red, where profits were higher than those in grey cotton production, and international markets were maintained for longer.

Cotton spinning and weaving was a great employer of low-skilled and badly-paid women and children, and was built on the back of a system of slave labour in North America. Machines quickly replaced skilled male workers, such as handloom weavers. It was an exploitative industry in many ways, reflected in high levels of trade union activity and frequent strikes, although it also pioneered new machine technologies and made a product that transformed working-class clothing for the better. The Turkey red industry was of a different character to mass-produced grey cotton manufacture. It used high technology in large and sophisticated working units, but it also employed a higher percentage of skilled male workers, from designers to pattern cutters, dyers and printers. By the mid-nineteenth century, when the Turkey red manufacturers had established their global trade and printed cottons were a ubiquitous part of Scottish and British clothing and household textiles, the industry was extensively engaged in chemical experimentation with new dyes and protected its intellectual property through design copyright. It was uniquely engaged in international market-information gathering through extensive networks of agents around the world, with one of the leading Scottish entrepreneurs in the sector making two lengthy trips to India to see the greatest export market at close quarters. Scottish Turkey red cottons were famous throughout the world for their quality, colour and design and the legacy of these textiles, and the vast industry that produced them can still be seen today.

William Stirling & Sons

Of the 'big three' Turkey red firms in the Vale of Leven, William Stirling & Sons was the first to establish itself in the area. A Glasgow merchant who commissioned printed cottons from London for sale in Glasgow and then moved into printing, dyeing and bleaching on his own account, founded the firm in Glasgow in the mid-eighteenth century. Stirling relocated to the Vale of Leven and founded the Cordale Works in the 1770s to take advantage of plentiful fresh water, good bleachfields and cheap labour.[7] The company purchased the Dalquhurn Works in 1789, which was a further fully operational calico printing establishment with three copperplate shops that also employed 200 'pencillers' who were responsible for brushing in blues and yellows by hand onto fabric. In the second generation of Stirling's ownership in the 1820s, the company expanded into Turkey red dyeing and printing, adopting and perfecting a technique which many Glasgow firms had failed to do. Third and fourth generations of the Stirling family were active in the business, but by the 1850s others had entered the partnership, including John Matheson, son of a calico printer and Turkey red dyer of Barrhead, and a significant innovator in the firm's history.[8]

By mid-nineteenth century, William Stirling & Sons was the largest and longest established firm of its type in Scotland; it occupied two distinct manufacturing sites in the Vale where it processed unbleached 'grey' cotton textiles woven in either Glasgow or Manchester. The Cordale Printworks and the Dalquhurn Dyeworks, on the banks of the Leven near the village of Renton, employed almost 1,500 workers in 1868, using state-of-the art technology housed in extensive, utilitarian shed-like buildings, with terraced workers housing nearby. One of the terraces that still survives, India Street, built by rival firm John Orr Ewing & Co., gives a hint of the industry's global horizons. Two-thirds of the workforce were women, many of Irish background, mostly engaged in the dyeing process, which was less skilled than printing where the workforce was mainly male. Irish women were also employed in the other Vale of Leven firms, with their presence in Dunbartonshire due to concerted efforts to attract 'strong girls willing to work' from southern Ireland.[9] Stirling's annual production, mostly for export, was almost nineteen million yards of cloth, about half of this plain dyed, the other half patterned, along with 800,000 lbs of dyed yarn for weaving elsewhere. The company also manufactured large quantities of patterned bandanna handkerchiefs, produced at a rate of 4,000 a day according to order. The extent of both the works, the workforce and the scale of production and export was such that William Stirling & Sons Turkey red factories were described in detail in a *Scotsman* article of 1868 by one of the first journalists to undertake a systematic industrial survey of Scotland.[10]

The different partners in William Stirling & Sons kept country houses in the vicinity of their Vale of Leven works or nearby in Helensburgh. They also lived part of the week in Glasgow because the commercial side of this business, and that of the other Vale of Leven Turkey red firms, was conducted from premises in central Glasgow, from where they managed their own sales rather than using merchant middlemen, which was usual in lower quality textile production.[11] Reflecting the growth of the industry, Stirling's commercial premises were extended in the late 1850s with the building of a new complex

Figure 1.2

Numbers 138–140 West George Street in Glasgow (middle building shown here) were occupied by William Stirling & Sons from the 1850s onwards. The corner building was a Clydesdale Bank which was built in 1867. Thomas Annan Collection, late 19th century.

© CSG CIC Glasgow Museums and Libraries Collection: The Mitchell Library, Special Collections

Figure 1.3

John Matheson (1817–78), a partner in William Stirling & Sons, was responsible for much of the firm's expansion in the mid-19th century. He twice visited India in the 1860s and 1870s. Image from *Memoirs and Portraits of One Hundred Glasgow Men* (Glasgow, 1886).

© Glasgow University Library. Licensor www.scran.ac.uk

of warehouse, salesroom and offices at 138–140 West George Street, designed by architecture practice Baird and Thomson in the 'modern Italian style, rich and dignified in appearance' and costing £5,500. This building [Fig. 1.2], over four floors with a street frontage of 62 feet, included a salesroom measuring 60 feet by 40 feet to the rear of the premises, with a high clear ceiling lit from the roof, and elaborate ornamented plasterwork. The front part of the building comprised basement storage and business rooms and counting houses on the three floors above the street, for the 'principals of the establishment', with seven front-facing windows on each floor, a richly decorated façade with scrollwork iron railings, and five ornamental gas lamps at regular intervals.[12] In the mid-1860s, the immediate neighbours in this part of Glasgow's commercial district included the offices of London-based dye manufacturers, Simpson, Maule & Nicholson, the inventors of magenta-based dyes and various commission agents, some of whose names feature in Stirling's order books. Another neighbour was S. Miller, 'wood engraver', who may have had some involvement in wood block pattern design for the Turkey red printing industry.[13]

John Matheson [Fig. 1.3], the active and younger partner of the firm of William Stirling & Sons, was responsible for commissioning the new Glasgow premises. He had entered the business in 1846, having previously worked as a clerk in the salesroom of the Glasgow cotton-brokers Kelly & Co., and also having a family background in printing and dyeing. He started his career with Stirling's in charge of its Glasgow salesroom and then moved on to the Vale of Leven works, which was largely under his management by the late 1850s, where he made many technical innovations and expanded output.[14] Matheson was interested in the commercial life of Glasgow, active as a director of the Glasgow Chamber of Commerce and was appointed President of the Chamber in 1872.[15] He wrote and presented papers on commercial and financial subjects to bodies like the Social Science Association and British Association.[16] He also took a detailed interest in the marketing of his printed cottons, sufficient enough to take a trip to India via the overland route in 1861, just before the opening of the Suez Canal, which he later published as a travel account with his observations on the dress, manners and industry of the people.[17]

William Stirling & Sons had strong trade links around the globe and particularly in India. One of the pattern books in the Museum's Turkey Red Collection contains letters and fabric samples which were sent to Stirling's in the 1850s and 1860s by agents and merchants in Bombay, providing detailed information on sales and market demand [Fig. 1.4]. The India influence is evident in many of Stirling's designs, which include the paisley cone, peacocks and dancing girls; but the British market was also served with some unusual designs, including a set with obvious masonic symbols arranged in patterns. Later markets included Sri Lanka, Burma, Singapore, Indonesia, the Philippines, China and Japan. All these markets were, of course, competitive, and being so close to the rival Orr Ewing firms provided many opportunities for industrial espionage and design theft by employees. The Bombay Pattern Book includes many samples of successful designs sold by rival companies, which were sent to William Stirling & Sons for copying. Indeed, the firm seems to have built much of its commercial success on deliberate design theft from Swiss or Manchester-made patterns, or from patterns produced closer to home by competitor companies in Dunbartonshire.

Like their main Manchester rival, the German-founded firm of Frederick Steiner & Co., along with the other two major firms in the Vale of Leven, William Stirling & Sons exhibited their products at a number of the great and international exhibitions in Britain and abroad. These events, which were visited by millions, were a showcase for new designs and production technologies and the best exhibits were rewarded with medals. At the Crystal Palace exhibition of 1851, Stirling's printed textiles for the India market were described as being

Figure 1.4

A page from the Bombay Pattern Book, which contains textile samples and notes on market conditions in India, sent by Bombay commission agents to William Stirling & Sons between March 1853 and December 1868. The notes attached to the samples on this page detail which merchant was selling each type of cloth and the retail price in the bazaar.

Paper and cotton; height 510 mm; width 330 mm

National Museums Scotland
A.1962.1266.31.6.P86

'sharp, clear, and [of] good execution' and having patterns which 'present the natives with repetitions of their ancient designs at a moderate price'. For the same exhibition, William Stirling & Sons produced an elaborately decorated 'exhibition handkerchief' containing an image of Britannia, views of the Crystal Palace, various exotic animals to represent the four corners of the globe, along with trains, boats and classical gods. It was described as being of 'questionable taste' in the *Glasgow Herald*.[18] Similar commemorative designs were produced for numerous different occasions at home and abroad in the decades that followed, and were also manufactured by the other Turkey red firms.

John Orr Ewing & Co.

John Orr Ewing, founder of the company that bore his name, was born in Stirlingshire in 1809 [Fig. 1.5]. As a young man he worked in Glasgow as a clerk for a calenderer, producing highly finished cotton and linen cloth, where he later became the firm's sales agent, which brought him into contact with the Turkey red products of the Croftengea Works in the Vale of Leven. With a partner, Robert Alexander, he acquired Croftengea in 1835 and was soon one of the major producers of Turkey red, expanding with the now increasing export demand for such wares. A report of 1839 in the *New Statistical Account of Scotland* described the company as employing 192 men, 142 women and 104 children, with an output of close to three million yards of printed goods per year. A list of Scottish calico printers in 1840 recorded John Orr Ewing & Co. as having one machine (possibly a cylinder printing machine), five presses (probably copper plate presses or lead plate presses) and 84 tables for block printing. Though big by any standards, they were not yet in the same league as the older firm of William Stirling & Sons, which at the same date had two machines, 17 presses and 140 tables.[19]

By 1845, when John Orr Ewing was still only in his thirties, he had made a sufficient fortune to leave the business and it passed into the sole ownership of his partner. Two managers at the Croftengea Works ran the firm, now known as R. Alexander & Co. Robert Alexander oversaw further expansion, including the purchase of the Levenfield Printworks from John Todd & Co. in 1850, but the firm faltered under the new management regime and John Orr Ewing resumed an active role in the business in 1860. By the 1870s, the workforce had risen to 1,600 and, with an annual wage bill of over £50,000, it was deemed the largest of such firms in Britain. In addition to enjoying a robust export market, of all the Vale firms, John Orr Ewing & Co. was known for its high quality design department. Design espionage by the other Vale firms was generally directed against John Orr Ewing, and of the estimated 1,200 Turkey red patterns that were registered for copyright by the three Vale of Leven companies between the copyright acts of 1842 and 1883, almost 75 per cent were registered by John Orr Ewing & Co.[20]

The firm's success greatly relied on John Orr Ewing's skill in employing outstanding technical experts who developed systems of production to overcome some of the innate difficulties of the delicate Turkey red process.

Figure 1.5

John Orr Ewing (1809–78), founder of John Orr Ewing & Co. which became the largest Turkey red manufacturer in the Vale of Leven. Image taken from *Memoirs and Portraits of One Hundred Glasgow Men* (Glasgow, 1886).

© Glasgow University Library Licensor www.scran.ac.uk

One of these was John Wylie, a colourist who mixed and prepared dyes for yarn and cloth. Having worked for Turkey red manufacturers in Lancashire as well as Scotland, Wylie is credited with having introduced to John Orr Ewing & Co. a method of dyeing which meant that Turkey red goods could be produced all year round. The new method, known as the 'Steiner Process', after the Lancashire-based German entrepreneur of the same name, whose firm was always the main rival to the Vale producers, allowed indoor drying of processed cloth. This meant that the previously seasonal production cycle – which only permitted full output during the summer, because of the reliance on outdoor drying – was smoothed to one of continuous production. When John Orr Ewing left his business in 1845, John Wylie, along with several other skilled workers, joined John Orr Ewing's brother Archibald in his new firm. This doubtless accounts in part for Archibald's swift success, and also the relative failure of Robert Alexander & Co.[21]

Another key technician was John Hyde Christie, a trained chemist who joined the firm as a young man when it was re-established under Orr Ewing management in 1860. He was John Orr Ewing's right-hand man and became a partner in the firm on the eve of John's death in 1878. Christie's interest and contribution lay in the development of artificial dyes, particularly the manufacture of artificial alizarin, which had been synthesised in Germany in the 1860s. This offered a cheap and consistent alternative to natural alizarin from madder root. Christie, along with other leading members of the Turkey red community, responded to German competition with the formation of the British Alizarine Company to protect British interests. Christie's son, also called John, continued this chemicals interest and was responsible for further developments in Turkey red dyestuffs in the early twentieth century.

John Orr Ewing & Co. was the most technically sophisticated of the three Vale firms and set a high store by its reputation for quality. But Turkey red dyeing and printing was a dangerous business. The production process required considerable heat to dry the dyed cloth and yarn; fires were frequent. In 1873 a fire broke out in one of the stove rooms at the Alexandria Works and despite the best efforts of the works own fire service, it spread so quickly that the whole building was burned to the ground. The dangers were well known, of course; just a few months before, John Orr Ewing had enquired about building a separate chamber to heat the air for the stoves to lessen 'the risk of burning'.[22] The complex and ever-changing chemical process and multiple machines were also a risk to workers. In 1881, John Christie wrote to a business contact about his concerns for some of the dyers, with some men suffering swollen and pustulated hands and arms from an unknown cause in the production process.[23] Child workers also suffered injuries, as in 1885 when a young girl by the surname of Paterson injured her hand when cleaning a machine that was still in motion. This was common practice according to a report, despite warnings that cleaning should only be carried out once the machines had stopped.[24]

Archibald Orr Ewing & Co.

Having trained at the firm of his brother John Orr Ewing, and benefiting from the guidance of experienced men such as John Wylie at the Croftengea Works, Archibald Orr Ewing set up his own Turkey red dyeing and printing works at Levenbank near Jamestown in 1845. On the other side of the river to his brother, Archibald quickly established a strong presence in the industry and within five years was shipping dyed and printed cotton cloth to Asia. In 1850, the firm expanded to include a yarn dyeing works at Milton, previously owned by John Todd & Co., and in 1866 the company purchased the Dillichip Works, downstream from Levenbank. James Barr, a pattern drawer at the Levenbank Printfield, was witness to the acquisitions and expansion. He described the area prior to purchase as no more than 'half a dozen houses, of not very imposing dimensions, but substantially built, and well kept, [which] with the addition of a broom drying shed, comprised the whole'. He went on to observe, 'much of the ground now covered with huge brick erections was then open grassy fields, partly for bleaching purposes, and partly as pasture for cattle'.[25] Employment inevitably expanded and from a workforce of about 800 when first acquired, the business had grown to over 2,000 workers by 1878. The impact of this growth was soon apparent in the Vale of Leven, which comprised a series of small village communities. When Archibald Orr Ewing & Co. acquired the Levenbank Works, there were workmen's houses for just 20 families. Archibald built tenement housing close to the works, along with schools and churches, and the boundaries between the villages merged. The arrival of the railway and telegraph to service the industry and the needs of its workers, also helped to transform this once rural area, as did an export profile that embraced the sale of goods in India, Greece, Singapore, Indonesia, Australia, New Zealand, Sri Lanka, Mozambique, South Africa, Iraq, Japan, Fiji and Burma.

Though founded by brothers, the two Orr Ewing firms were highly competitive. Archibald Orr Ewing & Co. was fiercely protective of the

Figure 1.6

Trade labels under dispute between Archibald Orr Ewing & Co. and John Orr Ewing & Co., 1879.

Glasgow University Archive Services, United Turkey Red Co. Ltd collection, GB0248 [UGD13/5/13/3/14]

labels and trademarks that were used in the packaging of their dyed and printed export cottons, and the trademarks themselves were often intricate works of art, designed to represent quality and to target specific markets. The trademarks, crucial where overseas merchants and retail customers were illiterate or unfamiliar with English, were copyright registered and of great importance to the textile export industry as a whole.[26] In 1877, Archibald Orr Ewing & Co. accused John Orr Ewing & Co. of using a distinctive elephant trademark in India, which they claimed they had registered in 1875 and had been using for 30 years before that [Fig. 1.6]. Court depositions were taken in Calcutta and Britain and the case rumbled on for years before John Orr Ewing & Co. was forced to concede that they had no right to use the elephant mark. The company agreed to stop doing so and to pay compensation.[27] Archibald Orr Ewing brought similar cases against other rival firms at home and abroad.

While both the Orr Ewing brothers were successful in the Turkey red industry, Archibald had the more prominent public profile. He used his accumulated manufacturing wealth to expand his interests beyond the Vale of Leven for both business and personal gain. In 1857 the company paid £18,000 for land in Glasgow between West Nile

Street and Renfield Street to build extensive warehouses, and in 1863 Archibald purchased the estate of Ballikinrain in Stirlingshire for himself and his family. He invested in numerous ventures, including railway and shipping companies, silver mines near Salt Lake City in America, and also, closer to home, the production of artificial alizarin. Archibald was a prominent figure in Glasgow society, on the boards of numerous charitable institutions and served as a justice of the peace and a member of the Glasgow Chamber of Commerce. He made a considerable personal contribution to the building of the new university on Gilmorehill in Glasgow, and about the same time in 1868, and probably connected, he fought and won the parliamentary seat for Dunbartonshire, which he held for 24 years. That led to a shift in his sphere of interests towards London. Archibald's contributions to public life were rewarded in 1886 when he became the first Baronet of Ballikinrain.[28] [Fig. 1.7].

Figure 1.7

Archibald Orr Ewing (1819–93), the younger brother of John Orr Ewing, established his own Turkey red manufactory in 1845 and quickly developed a strong business. Archibald became MP for Dunbartonshire in 1868.

© CSG CIC Glasgow Museums and Libraries Collection: The Mitchell Library, Special Collections

Archibald Orr Ewing died in 1893 and his firm did not thrive thereafter, despite the presence of two of his sons as managing partners. It was members of John Orr Ewing & Co. who rose to prominence following the formation of the United Turkey Red Company in 1898.

The United Turkey Red Co. Ltd

Though they were business rivals, and sometimes also locked in bitter court battles over copyright and design theft, competition between the Vale of Leven firms did not prevent them from taking collective action when it came to trade disputes with workers. Employer combinations were frequently used to keep wages under control, to undermine strike action and to punish trades union leaders through blacklisting. In 1872, for instance, John Orr Ewing & Co. wrote to William Stirling & Sons asking how much Stirling's paid their enginemen in the printing department. It seems the Orr Ewing engineman had asked for a rise, telling their employer that Stirling's paid more. This, needless-to-say, was not the case and was swiftly denied, so ending the enginemen's ambitions for higher pay.[29]

Attempts to gain exemptions for Turkey red producers from the restrictive conditions set by the Factory Acts in the early 1870s were argued in parliament by Archibald Orr Ewing on behalf of himself and his rivals, with whom he corresponded on the matter.[30] The rise of German manufactured artificial alizarin and its use in India generated collective court action to prevent the fraudulent sale of synthetic dyed cloth under 'authentic' Turkey red labels.[31] The threat from synthetic dyes also stimulated the joint formation of the British Alizarine Company Ltd.

The UTR, a merged company formed out of the three existing Vale of Leven Turkey red firms, was created in 1898 as a defensive measure against increasing competition from and in India, where protectionist measures in the form of import duties were starting to impact on the market for British goods. The new firm had its production base in the Vale of Leven, but decisions were frequently made from offices in Manchester, the heart of the British textile industry, where the commercial managers and sales agents were based.[32] The Board of Directors met in Glasgow, and included several partners from the earlier three firms, chaired by John Christie, but there was a growing gap between the works, the agents and the board, and much evidence of conflict. On its first formation, the combined UTR workforce in the Vale was 5,286, the largest group being adult women. The largest factory, with 45 per cent of the total workers in six factories, was the Alexandria dyeworks, formerly owned by John Orr Ewing & Co.[33] [Fig. 1.8]. The output of the business was increasingly focused on the dyeing of yarn for export, rather than the more valuable printed cloth. Short-time working was frequent due to poor orders. There were efforts in 1900 to collaborate with the Manchester-based Calico Printers Association, including the founding of joint sales offices in North Africa and Turkey. Moves were made to shift the Cordale

Figure 1.8

Factory workers from the Dillichip Works, early 20th century. Young women like these, who mainly worked in the dyeing shops, were known as 'jeely eaters' because their hands were permanently tinged with red.

Courtesy of West Dunbartonshire Libraries and Museums

Works to calico printing, replacing Turkey red, and additional works were acquired at Burnbrae and Millburn for indigo dyeing and black goods. Clearly there were heroic attempts to diversify away from Turkey red into other export markets and for a while the business seemed to flourish. Indeed, there was a striking show of the UTR's wares at the Glasgow International Exhibition of 1901, although the display was mainly of yarn rather than printed cloth.[34]

Yet despite the efforts of men such as John Christie Jnr, son of John Hyde Christie, who invented an improved, cheaper Turkey red process, the UTR could not compete with its Manchester rivals or with the relentless rise of cheap foreign production. In the 1930s and 1940s a number of the Vale of Leven works fell into disuse and the original Turkey red process was abandoned in 1936. Other dyeing processes were tried and three of the works were taken into government use during the Second World War for the production of waterproofing canvas, camouflage printing and the making of 'anti-gas capes for the forces'.[35] The Alexandria Works remained the largest and longest lived of the UTR factories, but even its diverse product ranges could not keep the company afloat. The UTR was taken over by the Manchester-based Calico Printers Association in 1960 and a year later the Alexandria Works finally closed [Fig. 1.9]. Very little remains today of this once flourishing industry. The factories were soon demolished and just a few of the associated buildings found other uses or survived. Only fragments remain to tell the story in the

Figure 1.9

Croftengea Printworks, Alexandria. This vast complex belonged to John Orr Ewing & Co., the largest of the Vale of Leven firms. The Alexandria works were the last to close in the mid-20th century. Oblique aerial photograph taken facing north-west. Aerofilms collection, 1927.

© RCAHMS (Aerofilms collection). Licensor www.rcahms.gov.uk

present – a street name here, such as 'India Street' on a row of workmen's houses, or a wall and gate there. New housing has been built on sites where whirring machines once stood, and the river, once red with pollution, is now clean and home to salmon and birds. Perhaps the greatest surviving testimony to the industry is the Turkey Red Collection of pattern books that is now housed in National Museums Scotland.

National Museums Scotland Turkey Red Collection

The Turkey Red Collection of 200 pattern books was acquired by National Museums Scotland following the demise of the United Turkey Red Company Ltd in 1960. The survival of such a large collection of textile pattern books from one industry is rare, since most volumes were destroyed when designs went out of production.[36] Although the numbers in the Museum's collection are unusual, they represent a fraction of the patterns that would have been produced during the life of the industry [Fig. 1.10]. Moreover, they do not represent the whole of the surviving volumes, since a handful of pattern books attributed to the Vale of Leven Turkey red firms are housed in the local museum in Dumbarton, there are some in the University of Glasgow Archives, and one, which was taken to Manchester by the

Figure 1.10

The size of the pattern books in the Turkey Red Collection varies greatly, but most contain hundreds of fabric samples. While some of the pattern books are still in their original 19th-century leather bindings, many had their binding removed before the collection was acquired in the early 1960s.

Courtesy of the 'Colouring the Nation Project'

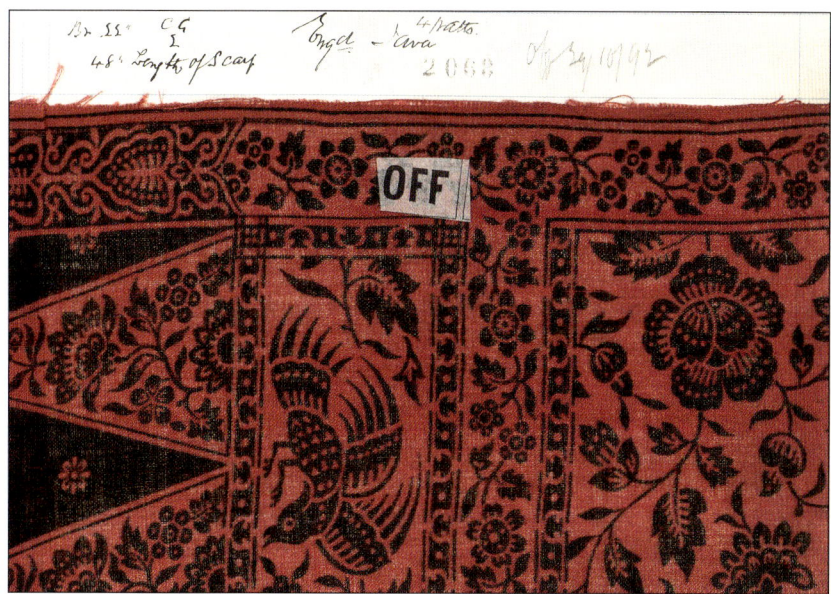

Figure 1.11

A textile sample which was intended for the Indonesian market. A pencil note above the sample says that it was taken 'off' on 29 October 1892. John Orr Ewing & Co., 1892.

Cotton; height 134mm; width 236mm

National Museums Scotland A.1962.1266.7.4.2068

Calico Printers Association in 1960, is now located in the museum of the Society of Dyers and Colourists in Bradford. Business papers for the same companies are in the Scottish Business Archive at the University of Glasgow and in the Manchester County Record Office.

It would take years to count exactly how many different fabric samples (or how many different designs) there are in the Museum's collection, but a rough estimate is 40,000 items, including Turkey red dyed and printed cotton samples and designs drawn or painted onto paper. Some of the pattern books are just small booklets with only one or two samples; others are huge leather-bound volumes containing hundreds of patterns. The size of the samples also varies – some are just a couple of centimetres long while others are almost a metre squared.

Most of the pattern books were used as manufacturing tools, kept as records of the designs a firm produced, with some also including notes on orders made and completed. The books were placed in different areas of a factory, for use as reference points by workshop managers. Many contain cryptic notations and marks that refer to the number of the pattern, the date it was created or used, or the type of cloth that was needed. When a design was taken out of production it was noted as cancelled [Fig. 1.11].

For ease of referencing, and reflecting the organization of printworks, many of the pattern books contain patterns produced by just one printing technique. So, for example, there are 16 'block' pattern books which contain designs produced mainly by hand block printing, one of the oldest textile printing techniques. There are also 'flat press' printed pattern books, 'lead plate' pattern books and 'cylinder' pattern books. Cylinder pattern books are the largest group, probably because cylinder printing, a development of the later nineteenth century, was the most efficient method of textile printing when compared with other techniques. If two printing methods were required to produce a single pattern – such as lead plate printing and cylinder printing – the pattern was given two numbers: one to indicate which lead plate should be used, and the second referring to the cylinder number.

A small number of the pattern books are what were called 'show books'. These were used in the salesrooms, or by salesmen in the field, to show customers and merchants the fully finished designs. There would have been many more books like this in the past, but since they were separated from the production process and factory premises, their survival has been poor. The show books, which can be identified from the higher quality bindings and gilt edgings, contain relatively large samples showing more of the finished design than was usual in workshop pattern books. The samples are numbered with gilt labels and are carefully arranged and pasted for a pleasing effect [Fig. 1.12]. Many of the samples in the workshop pattern books have skewed alignments where the printing process did not register properly, but this was not the case in the show books.

Another type of pattern books in the Museum's Turkey Red Collection comprises order books, which were probably kept in the Glasgow offices of the various Turkey red firms [Fig. 1.13]. These vary in character, but most contain dated fabric samples and some cost information for delivering specific orders, including labour costs. These books mostly date from the 1850s to late 1880s, when the

Figure 1.12

This large lead plate produced design is from a 'show book' which would have been used to demonstrate to potential customers and merchants which designs were available. A large, bold design like this would have been suitable for the South Pacific market. Probably produced by John Orr Ewing & Co. in the late 19th century.

Cotton; height 466mm; width 552mm

National Museums Scotland
A.1962.1266.12.10.1316

industry was at its peak. By the 1890s and the formation of the UTR merger, the industry was conducting much of its business through agents in Manchester and these order books have not survived. Reflecting the changing character of the business, however, part of the collection comprises four laboratory and dyestuffs recipe books with attached samples, which are testimony to the early twentieth-century endeavours by technical staff in the Vale of Leven to develop new synthetic dyes such as 'para red' and 'para orange'.

While we know that most of the pattern books were in use in the later decades of the nineteenth century, when Turkey red cotton production was at its peak, it is difficult to put specific dates on many of the volumes; labelling, where it does exist, was not consistent. The earliest dated book is from 1837 and contains block printed patterns generated by either William Stirling & Sons or John Orr Ewing & Co. The last of the dateable books is for 1940 and is one of the smallest in the collection, little more than a booklet with a couple of samples for the India market. Some books can be dated from their bindings or the stationer's labels, and in some cases, of course, the cryptic

Figure 1.13

A page from an order book of 1874. Each entry lists how much of the fabric was ordered and a breakdown of the costs involved in fulfilling that order. John Orr Ewing & Co., August 1874.

Paper and cotton, height 430 mm; width 345 mm

National Museums Scotland
A.1962.1266.76.6.552

notations include references to dates indicating when a particular cylinder or plate was first in production, or when they were re-engraved, suggesting a popular pattern with a long production run. Of course, many of the best-selling patterns were in production for decades and carried over with little or no change from one pattern book to another.

Not only has the dating been a challenge, attributing the pattern books to one or another firm has been difficult, mainly because such detail would not have been recorded at the time of creation when the pattern books were only ever intended to be seen by workers in their own place of work. Most of the books date from the mid- to late nineteenth century, which means they were produced and used by one of the three big Vale of Leven firms while they were still separate entities. But it is only when a volume includes letters, which is rare, or an indication of a specific factory or workshop premises, that a clear identification can be made. The largest group, comprising 55 pattern books, can be positively linked with John Orr Ewing & Co., which was the biggest of the three firms at the time of the UTR merger in 1898. John Orr Ewing & Co. was also the firm best known for high quality design, with the largest number of patterns registered for copyright, and its main business partner, John Hyde Christie, was Chairman of UTR when the merger first occurred. It seems likely, therefore, that the survival of so many pattern books from the former firm of John Orr Ewing reflected a UTR business decision to keep these patterns in production. One of the most interesting volumes is the small but informative Shanghai Pattern Book, which records a series of experimental consignments sent to the Far East in the 1860s on tea-clipper ships, many of them famous, in which it seems likely that John Orr Ewing may have had financial interests.

Only seven pattern books can be unequivocally connected with William Stirling & Sons, but this group includes the unique Bombay Pattern Book of 1853 to 1868, which is unusual for containing commission-agents' letters from Bombay alongside samples of patterns, many produced locally or by rival companies, with instructions for copying. Many more pattern books like this doubtless existed in each of the firms, but since they were maintained in the Glasgow offices and not in the Vale of Leven factory premises, their survival has been poor. Only five volumes have been clearly linked with Archibald Orr Ewing & Co., which was the shortest lived of the 'big three'. Other firms that can be identified in the collection include Todd & Co., R. Alexander & Co. and Anderson, Wright & Co., who were all absorbed into the three main firms in the mid- to late nineteenth century. The majority of volumes, however, remain unattributed.

Notes

1. Beverly Lemire, *Fashion's Favourite: The Cotton Trade and the Consumer in Britain, 1660–1800* (Oxford, 1991).
2. Giorgio Riello and Prasannan Parthasarathi (eds) *The Spinning World: A Global History of Cotton Textiles, 1200–1850* (Oxford, 2011).
3. Quoted by Lemire, *Fashion's Favourite*, p.16.
4. Anthony Cooke, *The Rise and Fall of the Scottish Cotton Industry, 1778–1914* (Manchester, 2010).
5. Francina Irwin, 'Scottish eighteenth-century chintz and its design', part 1, *The Burlington Magazine*, 107: 750 (1965), pp. 452–58.
6. David Bremner, *The Industries of Scotland: Their Rise, Progress and Present Condition* (Glasgow, 1869), 'Cotton manufactures'.
7. *Memoirs and Portraits of One Hundred Glasgow Men* (Glasgow, 1886), ch. 88, 'James Stirling, 1805–83'.
8. *Memoirs and Portraits*, ch. 63, 'John Matheson, 1817–78'.
9. University of Glasgow Archives (hereafter UGA): UGD13/1/8/229. Letter dated 19 Sept. 1873.
10. The series, by David Bremner, began on 27 Jan. 1868 and was subsequently published as *The Industries of Scotland: Their Rise, Progress and Present Condition* (Glasgow, 1869). See pages 297–304 for a detailed description of the Stirling Turkey red works.
11. See Stanley Chapman, 'The commercial sector', in Mary B. Rose (ed.), *The Lancashire Cotton Industry. A History Since 1700* (Preston, 1996), pp. 63–93.
12. *Building News*, 18 May 1860, p. 403. Historic Scotland Listed Buildings Register, ref. 33240.
13. *Glasgow Post Office Directory*, 1865–66, p. 371.
14. Joseph Irving, *The Book of Dunbartonshire: A History of the County, Burghs, Parishes and Lands, Memoirs of Families, and Notices of Industries Carried on in the Lennox District*, vol. 1 (Edinburgh, 1879), p. 361.
15. *Memoirs and Portraits*. Ch. 63. 'John Matheson, 1817–78.'
16. One lecture, given to the British Association meeting in Glasgow in 1876 and later published, was titled 'The Silver Dilemma': see *Memoirs and Portraits*, p. 221.
17. John Matheson, *England to Delhi: A Narrative of Indian Travel* (London, 1870).
18. *Glasgow Herald*, 21 February 1851.
19. *The Textile Colourist: A Monthly Journal of Bleaching, Printing, Dyeing and Finishing Textile Fabrics*, vol. 1 (Manchester, 1876), 'List of Scotch calico printers, 1840'.
20. See Chapter 3 in this publication.
21. UGA: UGD13/5/25 Archibald Orr Ewing & Co. versus John Orr Ewing & Co. Glasgow Sheriff Court, April 1877. Copy record.
22. UGA: UGD13/1/8/218. Letter dated 7 June 1873.
23. UGA: UGD13/1/8/477. Letter dated 7 April 1881.
24. UGA: UGD13/1/8/637. Letter dated 7 July 1885.
25. James Barr, *Balloch and Around: Life in Balloch, the Vale of Leven and Loch Lomondside, 1820–45* (Dumbarton, 1893), p. 30.
26. D. M. Higgins and Geoffrey Tweedale, 'The trade mark question and the Lancashire cotton textile industry', *Textile History* 27: 2 (1996), pp. 207–28.
27. UGA: UGD13/5/13/1: Bundle 1. Minute of Agreement dated 23 January 1879.
28. Anthony Slaven and Sydney Checkland (eds), *Dictionary of Scottish Business Biography, 1860–1960*, vol. 1 (Aberdeen, 1986).
29. UGA: UGD13/1/8/194. Letter dated 13 December 1872.
30. UGA: UGD13/1/8/130. Letter dated 3 February 1872.
31. *Times of India*, 28 August 1889.
32. Manchester County Record Office (hereafter MCRO): United Turkey Red Co. Ltd (hereafter UTR) Minute Books 1–4.
33. MCRO: UTR Minute Book 2, 7 June 1899.
34. MCRO: UTR Minute Book 2, 12 September 1900.
35. UGA: UGD13/5/22. Memorandum dated 10 March 1942.
36. Sally Tuckett and Stana Nenadic, 'Colouring the Nation: A new in-depth study of the Turkey red pattern books in the National Museums of Scotland', *Textile History* 42: 2 (2012), pp. 140–51.

CHAPTER TWO

Dyeing and printing

WE LIVE in a world today of seemingly endless varieties and shades of colour, with little popular understanding of how colour is created, or of how recent this bright and multi-coloured experience is. The modern interest in the use of 'heritage' colours in interior decoration informs some consumers of a more subtle or muted palette in the past and of the use of natural materials for generating colour. But the paint colours marketed by firms like Farrow & Ball reflect the decorative schemes once favoured by the wealthy and some of these colours are inventions for the present.

For most people in most periods and cultures before the nineteenth century, colour in textiles was limited and the colour of everyday clothing was simply that of the raw materials when woven. Tinted, bleached, or patterned fabrics, woven or printed, were a luxury. For labouring men and women in eighteenth-century Britain, their linen shirts and petticoats were described as being 'sad' coloured – that is a dull grey/fawn – which is natural to unprocessed linen and has the virtue of not showing the dirt.[1] In China, the peasants in some regions wore cotton clothing of a dusky yellow, which became fashionable in Europe in the eighteenth century and was known in the west as 'nankeen'. It was assumed that this was dyed, and the colour was reproduced in Europe, but in reality the colour was simply that which was natural to the locally grown plant, with pink-tinged varieties of cotton produced in other parts of the country.[2] Pure white linen, achieved through bleaching and frequent washing and starching, was expensive to produce and maintain and therefore a sign of status and the preserve of the rich throughout the eighteenth century.

Bright colours existed in all developed cultures of the past, with chemical techniques for fixing colour in fabric evolving alongside an understanding of the colour-generating potential of locally available natural dyestuffs. The brightest and deepest hues were always the most expensive, along with pure white and pure black, and the capacity of fabrics to accommodate bright colours varied, with plant-derived

Opposite page:

Finished sample of hand block printed cloth (see Fig. 2.6).

National Museums Scotland

cotton or linen reacting differently to animal-derived silk and wool. Much of the expense of the brightest colours in the pre-modern world arose from the reliance on imported dyestuffs – such as indigo for blue, which was widely traded for centuries, and always costly because it was difficult to grow and process. Early goods sent from India to eighteenth-century Britain were dominated in value by raw indigo, and indigo blue was a high status colour in China where it was more widely valued than red. Red, however, was always important, along with its close relations of pink and purple. Red and purple were the colours of cardinals and popes, of kings and queens and military leaders. Red is widely seen as the colour of love and power, of revolution and anger.

The cultural significance of red could vary from place to place and through time. According to one nineteenth-century commentary reflecting on 'colours and their meanings', the favouring of different colours is 'an exponent of the degree of civilization'.

> RED finds its fitness among savage races, and with underdeveloped natures.
> YELLOW indicates transition from barbarism to civilization.
> GREEN, advanced civilization.
> PURPLE, monarchical enlightenment, which is will individualised in but one. Modification and harmony [of colour] are only with people free to follow taste and select for themselves.[3]

The same American author, reflecting on the personal use of red in clothing, suggested:

> It is deemed evidence of immaturity for women in the fall time of life to sport crimson and scarlet and orange. Sober greys (which mean old, mature), quiet brown, and even sombre blacks, are rather what are looked for.

Here, as in other cultural expressions, red is associated with youthfulness and fertility or virility, whereas black is the colour of seriousness and dignity. The nineteenth-century widespread adoption of black, particularly in men's clothing, is commonly associated with the cult of seriousness. But the character and cost of dyestuffs was also partly responsible for this trend, since the cheapest dyed colour in nineteenth-century textiles – costing a fraction of natural red, blue or purple – was black made from a new source of dyes, imported logwood. Prior to this, black was expensive because it was made from blending the darkest indigo with deepest red madder, and those dyes were costly.⁴ So black represented a revolution in colour in the nineteenth century, and the comparable revolution in the twentieth century was probably the wide availability of white, made possible through new processes for dyeing cotton, the invention of synthetic fibres, modern washing powders and the domestic washing machine. The other colour that was costly in the eighteenth century, but became cheap with new dyeing technologies and natural sources after 1800, was yellow. Red, however, remained an expensive dyeing process throughout the nineteenth century before the complexities of the finest of the reds, known as Turkey red, was undermined by the cheap synthetic dyes that we mostly experience today.

The Turkey red process

The term 'Turkey red' applies not to the colour but rather to the *process* that was used to create the bright and fast red that is seen in the Museum's pattern book collection. The process was complex, repetitive and expensive, but the end product enjoyed a wide popularity and justified the cost. Indeed, Turkey red dyeing and printing was probably the most profitable of all the cotton finishing sectors in the nineteenth-century textile industry.

For centuries, British and European dyers had been seeking a bright red dye which could withstand strong sunlight and frequent washing without fading, and knowing of the Turkey red process – so-called because it was thought to have originated in that part of the eastern Mediterranean – they were keen to reproduce it. Skilled dyers in Holland and France first perfected the process in the west but were determined to keep the technique a secret; despite espionage expeditions and financial incentives from the Society of Arts in London, it was not adopted successfully in Britain until the 1780s, first in Manchester and then Glasgow.⁵

The Turkey red process involved multiple steps, could take weeks to complete and required almost constant attention from the workforce. The main component was madder, a plant root, of which there are many varieties, but the one most commonly used is called *Rubia tinctorum*, or 'dyer's madder'.⁶ A number of other ingredients was also required, including, as was common in many early chemical processes, rancid olive oil and sheep's dung, which were used for oiling and preparing the cloth before it was dyed. In 1845, one Peter Davie in the Vale of Leven, possibly working for William Stirling & Sons, was paid £1 10s 2d for spending twelve days tramping on large amounts of sheep dung, presumably to break it down for the solution that was used to soak the cloth.[7] During the actual dyeing of the cloth, the madder extract (alizarin) was combined with bullocks' blood. The blood seems to have been more for alchemical rather than any real purpose, but it was still in high demand. According to one account, William Stirling & Sons used 130,000 gallons of bullocks' blood a year[8] and it was even advertised by abattoirs in the local press as being particularly suitable for the Turkey red industry.[9] Supplies of bullocks' blood, which came in wooden barrels, were a constant source of irritation in Turkey red factories, particularly in the heat of the summer, generating frequent complaints, as in August 1887 when John Orr Ewing & Co. wrote to Messrs Lewes & Co. of Shettleston in the east end of Glasgow:

> We are much annoyed at your sending us Blood in casks which are unfit to hold anything. These casks are in the most wretched condition and if you send us any more like them we shall refuse to take delivery of the blood.[10]

Descriptions of the Turkey red process vary greatly, with some purposefully oblique, reflecting the secretive nature of the industry. The man who is credited with first bringing the process to Scotland, Frenchman Pierre Jacques Papillon, published his method for Turkey red dyeing and printing as part of an agreement with the Board of Trustees for Fisheries and Manufactures, in return for a financial incentive to remain in Scotland and develop his business. But his account was soon criticised for being 'complicated and incongruous … anomalies occur which would lead scientific persons to suppose that M. Papillon wished either wilfully to mislead the British public, or that he possessed no chemical science whatever'.[11]

In simplified terms, although this varied in its details from factory to factory, there were five main phases to the Turkey red dyeing process, applied initially just to cotton yarn and later to woven 'grey' cloth. The process was only really suitable for dyeing cotton, though occasionally it was also used on some wool cloth, because cotton as a yarn and textile is sufficiently robust to withstand the punishing multiple processes. The stages were:

- cleaning (or bleaching) the cloth or yarn to remove impurities and prepare it for the dyeing process (in the early stages of the industry this required prolonged periods of exposure to the air and sunlight, with the cloth being spread out on the ground);
- preparing the cloth or yarn by saturating it with rancid olive oil and sheep dung;

- mordanting the cloth or yarn with alum to ensure that the dyestuff would stick to the cloth;
- dyeing the cloth or yarn in vats containing the madder extract and the bullocks' blood;
- cleaning and brightening the cloth by boiling in a solution of chloride of tin.[12]

Each step was repeated frequently and the process could take up to 25 days. In one account written by Scottish industrial journalist David Bremner for the *Scotsman* newspaper, it was noted that the cloth was subjected to thirty 'preparatory operations' before it had even reached the mordanting stage.[13] The work was clearly labour intensive, often requiring nightshifts and weekend working to ensure continuity in the process. Endeavours to cut labour costs over the course of the nineteenth century were focussed on streamlining the production process to reduce the numbers of days involved. Gallons of water were required at each stage for repeated washings, boilings or immersions in dyes. For the Vale of Leven firms, the abundance of water from the fast-flowing River Leven was one of the main attractions of the area; the other attraction was space for the extensive sheds, drying greens, equipment and machinery that their businesses required. The industry could not be conducted effectively on a small scale, as Papillon confirmed in his report to the Board of Trustees in 1804. The 'number of vessels necessary for this business is greater in proportion to the extent of the manufactory', and some of the equipment, such as large copper vessels or wooden tubs and barrels hooped with copper (not iron, which effected the chemical process), were expensive.[14]

Mid-nineteenth century maps of the Levenside Turkey red works show massive complexes of purpose-built structures, each with their own particular function, such as dye houses, boiler houses, madder stores (necessary because the dyeing agent was delicate and susceptible to atmospheric damage), bleaching houses, wash wheel houses, engine houses, discharging houses, block printing and machine printing shops [Fig. 2.1]. The dye works of William Stirling & Sons employed 26 steam engines powered by 14 boilers, as well as the endless dye vats, washing machines (or dash wheels) and conveyor-belt mechanisms that moved the cloth around the works.[15] In 1873, the Barrowfield works of Henry Monteith & Co. (famous for its Turkey red bandannas) was advertised for sale. There was 28 acres of land, a print works with eight cylinder printing machines, 20 lead plate discharging presses, flat presses, an indigo dye works, and 'all necessary Buildings and Machinery for the Preparatory and Finishing Pro-

Figure 2.1

Detail of the town plan of Alexandria, showing the different buildings of the Croftengea Printworks. Wash houses, madder stores, dung stores and engraving shops are all contained within the boundaries of the works. Ordnance Survey, town plan Alexandria, sheet XVIII.9.10, 1859.

Reproduced by permission of the National Library of Scotland

cesses'.[16] Earlier accounts of the Barrowfield works, published in the 1830s and 1840s, described the discharging gallery where the famous bandannas were made. This room alone was 100 feet long, containing 16 presses, which were 6 feet high and 4 or 5 feet square.[17]

As a high-cost industry, Turkey red manufacturers were constantly looking for ways to improve, simplify or speed up their production process. Two years after the process was first introduced to Scotland, Papillon's business partner George Macintosh reduced the time needed to complete it from 25 days to 20.[18] Improvements made abroad in Europe were also imported to Scotland. Daniel Koechlin of Mulhouse, for instance, developed the first successful method for dyeing cloth in 1811 (not just yarn), which opened the way for the emergence of a more efficient dyeing and printing industry on one site.[19] The need to expose cloth to the open air at various stages of preparation and dyeing was also a limiting factor, particularly in west Scotland where rainy days were frequent; Papillon recommended using stoves for drying, which were expensive and susceptible to fires.[20] In the 1830s, a new indoor drying process was developed in Manchester by Frederick Steiner, German founder of a great Turkey red business, which the Scots subsequently adopted, allowing year-round production, though even in the 1870s yarn was still dried outdoors in the summer.[21] Large stoves with temperatures up to 180° were used at various stages during the dyeing process, with the drying stoves of John Orr Ewing & Co. in 1873 described as 80 feet long, 41 feet wide and 39 feet high.[22] With such high temperatures and flammable material around, it is not surprising that one of the greatest hazards in Turkey red production was fire, which all the Vale of Leven firms experienced, sometimes with loss of life. William Stirling & Sons had a particularly bad run of luck in 1876 when the firm suffered four significant fires in the space of six months.[23]

Although the Turkey red process was shortened and improved, it remained labour intensive, placing high demands on its workers. The introduction of Factory Acts to limit working hours was met with pleas for exemption from the Vale of Leven employers. Archibald Orr Ewing, giving evidence to a Factory Acts Commission in 1875, claimed that a shorter working day on Saturday, which was then being mooted, would be detrimental to the industry as a whole because of the need for constant supervision of the dyeing process. His point was well taken, though his further argument that a half-day on Saturdays would simply make the workforce idle generated less sympathy.[24] This last observation gives a telling indication of how the Turkey red owners viewed their workforce. The industry, employing thousands of skilled and well-paid workers, had poor labour relations. Strikes were frequent, as were lay-offs later in the century, and the Turkey red process was noxious and dangerous for all involved. The hands of the Turkey red workers were permanently tinged red, and since they mostly lived in close proximity to the Vale of Leven factories, in families where often all the adults worked for the same firm, with oppressive management regimes to ensure that the technical secrets of the dyeing and printing were protected, the businesses involved were viewed with scant affection. The impact on the natural environment was also problematical. A letter of 1908 to the County Clerk of Dunbartonshire, following an enquiry into extensive pollution of the River Leven, included the following observations from the general manager of the United Turkey Red Company Ltd, which highlighted the disadvantages of the riverbank site in a new era of legislative control of factory effluent, and the costs entailed:

> In most of the effluents there are traces of suspended and colouring matters. Free acid is not present in the effluents from any of our works, all of them being practically neutral and perfectly harmless. The low level at which most of the Works are situated has made our task much more expensive, and difficult, than would been there had the works been situated on a higher level, but we claim that the

method settling now employed by us – the result of continued effort and experiment – is the best possible system which under the circumstances can be employed where the enormous volume of water is a primary factor.[25]

Printing methods

There are many methods for printing textiles: some relatively recent inventions and the result of technological developments in the late eighteenth and early nineteenth centuries, others in existence for thousands of years. Each printing method has its own advantages – some are quick to execute, others are cheap and cost effective, with certain techniques being the only ones possible in the production of a particular type of pattern.

There are four main ways of generating a pattern on fabric:

- Mordant printing – where a substance known as a mordant is first applied in patterns to the cloth before it is dyed. The mordant (also known as a fixing agent) combines with the dyestuff and the textile fibre, leaving an insoluble colour. Not all dyestuffs require a mordant, but madder, the main component in Turkey red, does.
- Direct printing – where colour is transferred directly onto the cloth to produce a pattern. Wood blocks, copper rollers and screens are examples of different techniques for direct printing.
- Discharge dyeing, though not technically a printing method, is still used to produce a pattern on cloth. The cloth is dyed and then a bleaching agent is used to remove or 'discharge' the colour from certain areas, creating the desired pattern.
- Resist dyeing is where a substance applied to the cloth in patterns is used to resist the dyestuff, so that only certain areas of the fabric can take on the colour. Batik dyeing is an example of this method, with wax employed to prevent the dyestuff from penetrating the cloth. Another is tie-dyeing, which involves pieces of string tied tightly around small parts of the cloth, which again prevents the dye from reaching the fibre.

All of these methods were used by the Vale of Leven Turkey red firms, and, as the Museum's pattern book collection shows, multiple methods were commonly applied to a single piece of fabric to create some of the more complex patterns. Although the typical mordants used in the Turkey red process were oil and alum, which when applied to certain areas of the cloth produced a pattern, a range of mordants could also be used at the same time, each reacting differently with the alizarin to produce varying shades of red as well as brown or black.[26]

Of the direct printing techniques, block printing is the oldest; it is thought to have originated in Persia or Egypt, before being perfected in India and later adopted in Europe.[27] Block printing was therefore the first to be used on any scale in Britain and was employed in printing on calico, wool and linen, as well as Turkey red cotton. The required design would be carved into a block of hard wood, such as holly, leaving the pattern in relief. If the pattern required different colours, say blue or green detail in a peacock, different blocks would be used for each colour. If fine lines were needed for small details such as flowers or birds' feet, then copper strips could be hammered into the block.[28] Each block was made with 'pitch pins', which were used to register the blocks and ensure that colour was transferred to the correct position on the cloth. The size of the wooden block would depend on the size of the pattern, but the blocks could not be too big as they would have been too heavy for the printer to lift. According to one account, the blocks used by the Scottish Turkey red firms were typically ten inches long by five inches broad.[29] Those used in India by craft printers were smaller [Fig. 2.2].

John Matheson, head of William Stirling & Sons, described the working methods of Indian craftsmen that he witnessed during his visit to India in 1861:

Figure 2.2

A cloth stamper from western India c.1870, using a small wood block to produce a repeated pattern down the length of the cloth. Some of his blocks are displayed in front. The man on the far right appears to be 'tieing' cloth for tie-dyeing. A photograph by Shivashanker Narayan, 1873, from the Archaeological Survey of India Collection.

© The British Library Board

The various orders of tradesmen – pipe makers, men-milliners, toy-manufacturers, and the rest, usually seated in tailor fashion, were at work in their respective shops, many of them in the precise position of huge window figures. Even dyers and calico printers plied their trade within these narrow recesses, one end of the room constituting the dye-work, and the other the print shop. The work of the former … is effected by dipping the cloth in pots of clay or brass containing a supply of the requisite liquors; that of the latter is accomplished through the instrumentality of tiny wooden blocks, on which the patterns are cut, the printing table being a board sustained on the crossed legs of the operator![30]

Figure 2.3

An example of the block printing technique in 18th-century Britain. Unlike the Indian craftsmen who sat down, British printers stood and moved down the length of the table, applying the block carefully to the cloth. An 18th-century engraving, English School.

Private collection/The Bridgeman Art Library

In striking contrast to India, in the Vale of Leven print shops 30-foot-long tables were used for the block printing [Fig. 2.3]. A length of cloth would be laid out along the table and the block printers, who worked in pairs, moved down the cloth, carefully lining up the block to the fabric to produce the pattern. The colours would be in a tub or bucket by the side of the table and were applied to the block when required. A young boy, called a 'tearer', would spread the coloured paste evenly over a piece of framed cloth for holding the dye and the printer would then place the block on the framed cloth to pick up the colour for transfer to the textile length. Once loaded with colour, the printer placed the block on the fabric and used a heavy mallet or 'mell' to strike it and secure an even print [Fig. 2.4]. The first colour had to dry before a second was applied. It was a skilled occupation with a long apprenticeship, and though labour intensive and expensive, block printing remained important throughout the life of the Turkey red industry. Blocks were normally cut on the manufacturers' premises to protect designs from theft. Sixteen of the surviving pattern books in the Museum's Turkey Red Collection can be identified as block printed pattern books, the earliest in use from the 1830s, whilst others belonged to the early twentieth century. Unfortunately, very few of the actual blocks still exist and at the formation of the United Turkey Red Co. Ltd in 1898, when production was severely rationalised, there was a deliberate destruction of many discontinued wood blocks and engraved lead plates, the latter sold to realise the value of the lead[31] [Figs. 2.5 and 2.6].

Printing with copper plates was first invented in the mid-eighteenth century and the principle was much the same as block printing, except that the design was etched into copper rather than engraved in relief on wood blocks. Copper plates allowed much finer designs than blocks, on larger surfaces, giving rise to bigger and more intricate designs. They were used by the Scottish Turkey red firms to generate fine black detail over white or red areas of fabric and were particularly important for handkerchief designs.

Cylinder printing, the next step from copper plate printing, effectively revolutionised the industry and was first patented by Thomas Bell of Glasgow in 1783. Designs were carved onto copper cylinders or rollers, which were mounted on a large central cylinder. Each cylinder was fed with its own colour as the cloth was passed through, with multi-coloured patterns achieved through the use of multiple cylinders. Each cylinder was about five or six inches in diameter and multiple cylinders and colours could print simultaneously. According to one account, a single machine with multiple cylinders could produce 15 yards of printed fabric a minute.[32] Another estimated that one cylinder machine, worked by one man and one tearer, could produce as much as 100 men and tearers with wood blocks or copper plates[33] [see Fig. 2.7].

Figure 2.4 (opposite, below)

A hand block printers' mell for striking a wood block to get an even print on the cloth; it was used in the Levenbank printworks, Vale of Leven in the late 19th century.

Courtesy of Rev. E. Houston

Figure 2.5 (left)

A rare surviving section of a hand block made of wood, engraved for Archibald Ewing & Co. in the late 19th century. The fabric sample in Fig. 2.6 shows the finished product.

Courtesy of West Dunbartonshire Libraries and Museums

Figure 2.6 (below)

Finished sample of hand block printed cloth. Archibald Orr Ewing & Co., late 19th century.

Cotton; height 250mm; width 236mm

National Museums Scotland
A.1962.1266.31.14.1875

Figure 2.7

Interior of the Dalmonach printworks of James Black & Co., Vale of Leven, later a concern of the Calico Printers Association. Each cylinder in this complex, state-of-the art machinery, would have been used to produce a different colour on a single pattern. Date 1867.

Courtesy of West Dunbartonshire Libraries and Museums

David Bremner, the industrial journalist who visited the Turkey red works of William Stirling & Sons in the late 1860s, noted that cylinder printing had one disadvantage in that it could only be used where the design was repeated through the length of the fabric. This reduced the utility for Turkey red firms who produced many designs for sari pieces and scarves where the end patterns and borders were different to the filling patterns.[34] Yet despite this limitation, printing with cylinders was important and particularly used in the production of cheaper fabrics, as indicated in the following monthly output data for John Orr Ewing & Co. in February 1887.

313,500 yards of cylinder printed cloth
150,000 yards of flat press printed cloth
57,000 yards of block printed cloth
22,500 yards of lead plate printed cloth[35]

Reflecting this output, most of the pattern books in the Museum's Turkey Red Collection contain patterns which were produced either all or in part by cylinder printing.

As this production data reveals, lead plate printing was a relatively small feature of John Orr Ewing and Co.'s output in the later nineteenth century. It is not technically a printing process at all, since extra colour is not imparted or transferred onto the cloth, but rather the colour is 'discharged' from already-dyed cloth through the use of bleaching agents applied via lead plates. The discharge process had been important in the earlier history of the Turkey red industry and was particularly associated with the production of bandanna handkerchiefs by companies like Henry Monteith & Co. The actual colour achieved in the discharge process depended on the solution that formed the discharging agent – a mixture of sulphuric acid and chloride of lime was used to produce white areas, while chromate of lead produced yellow areas.[36] The technique involved two plates of lead, with the required patterns carved into each plate. The plates were clamped together with the cloth between them, and the discharging liquor was passed through the plates; where it came into contact with the cloth, the colour was bleached away to leave a pattern, most commonly of spots and stripes[37] [Figs. 2.8 and 2.9]. The white or yellow areas left by the discharge process were sometimes overprinted with

Figure 2.8

A stained-glass window by Stephen Adam showing a lead plate press. Lengths of cloth were clamped between the lead plates and a discharge agent would be passed through them. Where the liquid contacted the cloth it would discharge the dye. This window is part of a series which celebrates workers and industries in the Maryhill area of Glasgow.

© CSG CIC Glasgow Museums Collection

Figure 2.9

The lead plate process was used to produce bandannas, a key feature of the early Turkey red industry. Lead plates were also used to create bold, simple designs such as the one above. John Orr Ewing & Co., 1870s–90s.

Cotton; height 138 mm; width 305 mm

National Museums Scotland A.1962.1266. 12.10.1027

cylinder or copper plate details for handkerchiefs or shawls. As with cylinder printing, lead plate printing could produce more finished textiles than the traditional block printing method because multiple handkerchiefs could be clamped together. Bremner estimated that the six presses run by six men in William Stirling & Sons' works in the 1860s produced 4,000 handkerchiefs in a ten-hour day.[38]

The term 'flat press printing', which figured significantly in the later nineteenth century, had ambiguous meaning within the Vale of Leven Turkey red firms. For the wider textile industry it referred to a semi-mechanised process, which used a system of engraved plates mounted on rails that moved along the length of the cloth in a similar motion to block printing.[39] The plates were made of copper, and the pattern, typically only in one colour, could be finely executed. Yet an account written by John F. Christie, manager in the United Turkey Red Co., noted that flat press machines 'were used mainly for discharge work – to put the white in the red and pink alizarin dyeing and so produce the genuine red, pink and white handkerchiefs for the home market and the large squares for the Indian one'.[40] He went on to say that different discharge presses were used for lead plate printing, which produced large bold patterns, mainly for export to the South Pacific. This would suggest that flat press printing was a discharge method, similar to, but distinct from, lead plate printing. Christie's description also suggests that flat press printing was used for such patterns as the 'two red' designs, where two shades of red and pink were produced on the same fabric, typically in floral patterns for furniture uses. There are five flat press printing pattern books in the Museum's Turkey Red Collection, three of them linked to Archibald Orr Ewing & Co. and one to John Orr Ewing & Co. [Fig. 2.10].

The final method of printing employed by the Vale of Leven Turkey red manufacturers was batik printing, a traditional method from Indonesia of what is known as pattern dyeing – where the pattern is produced through dyeing the cloth rather than direct printing. Typi-

Figure 2.10

Border design which shows the 'two red' colouring and white detail. John Orr Ewing & Co., early 1890s.

Cotton; height 230 mm; width 280 mm

National Museums Scotland A.1962.1266.3.3.2951

cally wax is used to prevent the dye from reaching certain areas of the cloth, but since cold wax is brittle, it allows small veins of colour to penetrate through to the fabric, giving the desired 'batik' crinkled look. Like the lead plate printing process, the white areas left behind were often over-printed with blocks or cylinder. There is a single pattern book in the Museum's collection from the early twentieth century, labelled 'Alexandria Batiks', containing patterns that were probably intended for the Javanese or West African market. When the UTR was created in 1898, and many printing processes were discontinued, what were termed 'Batick styles' were retained due to their profitability.[41]

The rise of synthetic dyes

The Scottish Turkey red industry was based on a sophisticated but traditional dyeing process using natural materials. Madder root, which was grown and processed in France and the Netherlands, was expensive, but also produced the brightest of reds. The active component of madder was the chemical substance known as alizarin, which was isolated and described by European chemists in the early nineteenth century.[42] Other chemical components of natural madder were identified and applied by the mid-nineteenth century, including purpurin, which produced a delicate lilac colour, and green alizarin, which was patented in Britain and famously displayed at the 1867 Paris International Exhibition.[43] But given the high cost of dyeing and printing with extracts of madder, the search was on to identify a new and cheaper synthetic source of alizarin.

Attempts to make an artificial version of natural madder were carried out in many dyeing firms in Britain, and the Scottish Turkey red companies employed university-trained chemists from an early date. Alizarin was finally synthesised in 1868 by German chemists, and German and English companies soon began producing this crucial ingredient for inclusion in the Turkey red process, where it quickly replaced natural madder extract. John Orr Ewing & Co. first introduced this artificial dyeing compound to Scotland in the 1880s.[44] Artificial alizarin generated a simpler, faster and more consistent dyeing process that reduced labour costs, and because it required less oiling and mordanting, and less soap for cleaning, material costs were also reduced.[45] However, the 'natural' method of dyeing still enjoyed the highest prestige and prices, and 'authentic' Turkey red from the Vale of Leven factories continued in production well into the twentieth century.

Although the first synthetic dye – i.e. picric acid, which produced a bright yellow on silk – was invented in 1771, the man widely regarded as responsible for the rise of synthetic dyes was William Henry Perkin (1838–1907).[46] In 1856, when still a chemistry student in London, Perkin, who was trying to synthesize the anti-malarial drug quinine from coal tar, accidentally discovered the first major aniline or coal-tar derived dye. A black residue that formed during his experiments, when dissolved in methylated spirit was found to produce a purple solution that worked well on silk. The colour of the dye, which came to be known as 'mauve', was entirely new and caused a sensation.[47] As an industrial novice, Perkin took advice from the textile industry, including Pullars of Perth, bleachers and dyers, and John Hyde Christie, the chemist and general manager of John Orr Ewing & Co., on the commercial development of mauve.[48] It became popular in high fashion uses, with royal patronage from Empress Eugénie of France and Queen Victoria, but synthetic mauve was always expensive.[49] Though limited in its applications, the potential presented by coal-tar waste from the ever increasing numbers of gas works in Britain and Europe, sparked a frenzy of activity among research chemists in industrial employment and in university departments, leading quickly to further synthetic colours such as magenta and green.

The new synthetics had two advantages over natural dyes. The first was cost and the second was consistency. Natural root products such as madder extract varied from batch to batch according to the growing and storage conditions. Indeed, madder powder was so easily damaged by exposure to light and atmosphere that the transportation was expensive.[50] Pattern books in the Museum's Turkey Red Collection, and the Bombay Pattern Book in particular, underline the importance of consistent colour quality from batch to batch of prints sent to the Indian market, but variations using the traditional dyeing method were inevitable. The use of artificial alizarin rather than natural madder still required the same many repetitive steps as before, but it was cheaper. The natural Turkey red process was not immediately superseded, however, and 'authentic' labelled goods that highlighted the natural dyeing process continued to enjoy a premium in the market-place.

German chemical companies led the way in artificial alizarin production and sales, but by the early 1880s the British Turkey red industry was fighting back with endeavours to restrict the use of this foreign commodity and the creation of the British Alizarine Company Ltd, whose directors included Archibald Orr Ewing and John Hyde Christie of John Orr Ewing & Co.[51] Christie's son, another chemist, led Scottish attempts to further improve natural Turkey red and alizarin dyeing, but the European dyestuffs companies were adept at developing not only their cheaper products with consistent results, but they also provided technical advice and services for their clients, which meant that dyeing and printing businesses were able to cut the costs of specialist staff at their works.[52] The penetration of German dyes into the Indian market came at a time when imperial policies of industrial restriction were increasingly seen as politically unacceptable and the impact on Scottish Turkey red producers was inevitable. The fight for market position in India gave rise to the founding of the United Turkey Red Company Ltd in 1898, but by this stage all of the companies involved in the merger were themselves major users of artificial dyes. The Dalquhurn works in 1898 produced yarn dyed in Turkey red and alizarin red, along with aniline versions of purple, green, orange, blue, pink, yellow and maroon. It was also starting to use a new type of artificial red, called 'para red', which was first invented in Germany 1889 and eventually replaced artificial alizarin.[53] In 1912, napthol reds superseded para reds.[54] The UTR, based mainly in the Vale of Leven, continued to maintain a chemical development division, and in the 1920s was conducting trials on the artificial dyestuff known 'Hydron blue', which was the rival to indigo blue.[55] But companies such as this could not compete with the great chemical giants that now dominated the dyestuffs industry. Traditional Turkey red dyeing and printing in the Vale of Leven eventually ceased production in 1936; and though the United Turkey Red Co. Ltd continued to manufacture other types of printed and dyed cottons, its market position slowly ebbed away before final closure in 1960.

Notes

1. John Styles, *The Dress of the People: Everyday Fashion in Eighteenth-Century England* (London, 2007).
2. 'A day at the Barrowfield dyeworks, Glasgow', *The Penny Magazine of the Society for the Diffusion of Useful Knowledge*, 13 (1844), pp. 289–93.
3. *The Continental Monthly: Devoted to Literature and National Policy*, August 1864.
4. Alexander Engel, 'Colouring markets: The industrial transformation of the dyestuff business revisited.' *Business History*, 54:1 (2012), pp. 10–29.
5. Naomi Tarrant, 'The Turkey red dyeing industry in the Vale of Leven', in J. Butt and K. Ponting (eds), *Scottish Textile History* (Aberdeen, 1987), p. 39.
6. Robert Chenciner, *Madder Red: A History of Luxury and Trade, Plant Dyes and Pigments in World Commerce and Art* (Richmond, 2000), p. 22.
7. UGA: UGD 13/4/4. Wages book, 1845.
8. David Bremner, *The Industries of Scotland: Their Rise, Progress and Present Condition* (Glasgow, 1869), p. 300.
9. *Glasgow Herald*, 14 February 1862.
10. UGA: UGD 13/1/8/666. Letter dated 6 August 1887.
11. George Macintosh, *Biographical Memoir of the Late Charles Macintosh, FRS of Campsie and Dunchattan* (Glasgow, 1847), p.121.
12. Accounts of the process can be found in 'A day at the Barrowfield Dyeworks'; *Chambers' Encyclopaedia* (1867); Bremner, *Industries of Scotland*.
13. Bremner, *Industries of Scotland*, p. 300.
14. Pierre Jacques Papillon, 'Method of dyeing cotton yarn a fixed Turkey red', *The Repertory of Arts, Manufactures and Agriculture*, vol. iv, (London, 1804), pp. 105–10.
15. Bremner, *Industries of Scotland*, p. 301.
16. *Glasgow Herald*, 22 December 1873.
17. Andrew Ure, 'Description of the Great Bandana Gallery in the Turkey red factory of Messrs Monteith and Co. at Glasgow', *The Glasgow Mechanics' Magazine and Annals of Philosophy*, (Glasgow, 1831), pp. 7–10; 'A day at the Barrowfield Dyeworks', p. 292.
18. Letter from George Macintosh to Charles Macintosh, 18 January 1787, cited in *Biographical Memoir of the Late Charles Macintosh*, p. 22.
19. Tarrant, 'Turkey red dyeing industry in the Vale of Leven', p. 41.
20. Papillon, 'Method of dyeing cotton yarn', p. 110.
21. Archibald Orr Ewing's testimony to the Factory Acts Commission, published in *Glasgow Herald*, 9 September 1875.
22. UGA: UGD 13/1/8/218. Letter dated 7 June 1873.
23. *Glasgow Herald*, 2 October 1876.
24. *Glasgow Herald*, 9 September 1875.
25. MCRO: UTR, Glasgow. Minute Book no. 4, 7 April 1908.
26. John R. Hume, 'Calico printing in the west of Scotland', *Seeing Red: Scotland's Exotic Textile Heritage*, p. 13.
27. Jennifer Harris (ed.) *Textiles: 5000 Years* (London, 1993), p. 37.
28. Archibald M. Aitken, 'Recollections of the Turkey red industry'. Unpublished manuscript written by a former UTR printer, 1996 (Private Collection). See also Harris, *5000 Years of Textiles*, p. 37.
29. Bremner, *Industries of Scotland*, pp. 302–3
30. John Matheson, *England to Delhi: A Narrative of Indian Travel* (London, 1870), pp. 359–60.
31. MCRO: UTR Minute Book 1, 6 April and 27 April 1898.
32. Bremner, *Industries of Scotland*, p. 303.
33. Anthony Cooke, *The Rise and Fall of the Scottish Cotton Industry, 1778–1914* (Manchester, 2010), p. 129.
34. Bremner, *Industries of Scotland*, p. 303.
35. UGA: UGD13/1/4, Minute book of John Orr Ewing & Co., 1887–88.
36. R. A. Peel, 'Zenith of alizarin prints: Impact of new ideas and dyes on the old craftmanship', *The Dyer and Textile Printer*, (July 1956), p. 119.
37. For contemporary accounts, see Ure, 'Description

38 Bremner, *Industries of Scotland*, p. 304.
39 Aitken, 'Recollections of the Turkey red industry'.
40 John F. Christie, cited in Peel, 'Zenith of alizarin prints', p. 119.
41 MCRO: UTR Minute Book 1, 6 April and 27 April 1898.
42 R. A. Peel, 'Perkin and the Scottish alizarin dyers', *The Dyer and Textile Printer* (May, 1956), pp. 851–54, p. 851.
43 Anthony S. Travis, 'Between broken root and artificial alizarin: Textile arts and manufacturers of madder', *History and Technology: An International Journal*, 12:1 (1994), pp. 1–22.
44 R. A. Peel, 'Alizarin users defy a threat', *The Dyer and Textile Printer* (June 1956), pp.1013–14.
45 Anthony S. Travis, *The Rainbow Makers: The Origins of the Synthetic Dyestuffs Industry in Western Europe* (London, 1993), p. 192.
46 Amy Butler Greenfield, *A Perfect Red: Empire, Espionage, and the Quest for the Color of Desire* (New York, 2005), p. 225.
47 Travis, *The Rainbow Makers*, p. 36.
48 Cooke, *Scottish Cotton Industry*, p. 128; R. A. Peel, 'Artificial alizarin users defy a threat', p. 1013.
49 Alexander Engel, 'Colouring markets: The industrial transformation of the dyestuff business revisited', *Business History*, 54:1 (2012), pp. 10–29.
50 Travis, *Rainbow Makers*, p.14; Chenciner, *Madder Red*, ch. 15; Greenfield, *A Perfect Red*, p. 228.
51 *Glasgow Herald*, 6 October 1882.
52 Engel, 'Colouring markets'.
53 UGA: UGD 13/5/4 Production records 1898–1902, United Turkey Red Co. Ltd.
54 Peel, 'Zenith of alizarin prints', p. 119. See also Tarrant, 'Turkey red dyeing', p. 45.
55 National Museums Scotland: Turkey Red Collection. Recipe book with recipes and trials for synthetic dyes. Accession no. A.1962.1266.77.3.

CHAPTER THREE

Design, copyright and exhibition

THE PRINTED cotton industry was a design-based industry, with product and market decisions based on a sophisticated understanding of changing fashions, awareness of the cultural meanings of design motifs and colours, technical innovation in printing techniques and a close eye to the activities of rival companies. Some of National Museums Scotland's Turkey red pattern books, and the Bombay Pattern Book in particular – which consists of a series of letters from commission agents in Bombay monitoring sales and placing orders with William Stirling & Sons – comprise a detailed engagement with the market demand for different designs. In June 1865, for instance, the Bombay firm of Ewart, Latham & Co. reported that 'zigzag patterns' were 'much liked', and this, it appears, was consistent with traditional Indian designs that were generally favoured in India. Or, in August 1866, and again reflecting long-held cultural preferences, the firm of Herman Lucius & Co. sent samples of Swiss chintz prints, stating 'if in pattern no. 6 yellow were substituted for black it would be an improvement; 40–50 cases could easily be sold during the season'.[1]

Much of what was produced in the Scottish Turkey red industry was traditional designs for conservative markets like India, with many prints remaining in production for decades. But there was design innovation, and the different firms employed designers and pattern drawers. Moreover, the textile industry more generally was involved in a sustained debate during the course of the nineteenth century over the issue of design education in Britain. Many companies, including those that feature in the Museum's Turkey Red Collection, sought to protect their best designs through copyright registration and through punitive employment practices to prevent workers removing samples from factories. The weakness of the law when it came to safeguarding intellectual property such as original design is highlighted by the numerous court cases over alleged design theft in cities like Glasgow and Manchester, but these cases also give

Opposite page:

An intricate design for cylinder printing (see Fig. 3.4).

National Museums Scotland

an insight to the design process. Textile manufacturers were notable exhibitors of their wares and the Great Exhibition movement in Britain and abroad provided numerous opportunities for firms to showcase their best products and designs, as well as their technical innovations in areas like printing and dyeing, and put them forward for prizes.

Textile designers

Designers for the textile industry in all its different areas, including printing, weaving and sewing, were of two distinct types. There were those who worked independently, had artistic credentials and status, and designed for a range of industries as well as being engaged more broadly in the fine arts. This 'freelance' group, which included many foreign artists, particularly French, was relatively small, whereas the second type of designer comprised the much larger group of mainly locally born, full-time employees and apprentices who worked exclusively for one firm. Almost no direct information survives for the names of the designers who worked for the three Vale of Leven companies whose pattern books form the Museum's Turkey Red Collection [Fig. 3.1]. Where information does exist, it is simply the fleeting inclusion of a name: such as that of 'James Lindsay' who signed one design in an undated pattern book now owned by West Dunbartonshire Council. Or, from a rare surviving wage book for 1845, there is mention of four 'drawers', probably meaning 'pattern drawers', headed by the highest paid worker in the list of all workers in the factory, William Brock, probably a designer, who earned £8 a month.[2]

Many pattern designers were the sons of pattern designers. One whose career is well known, because of his later celebrity as an artist of Scottish landscapes and genre scenes, is Tom McEwan (1847–1914) whose father was foreman pattern designer at Inglis & Wakefield, a Manchester firm that had a calico printing works at Busby near Glasgow. The family moved to Glasgow in 1859 and McEwan, aged twelve, began a seven-year design apprenticeship with Todd & Higginbotham, another Glasgow firm with Manchester connections. In 1873, aged 26 and after 14 years working in the textile industry, McEwan, who had been steadily developing his artistic interests as an amateur, gave up pattern designing to work full time as a painter. He exhibited extensively in Scotland and London, was commercially successful, and served several terms of office as President of the Glasgow Art Club in the later nineteenth century.[3]

Occasionally, newspapers offer an insight into the process of

Figure 3.1

Although there is little direct information about the designers, the Turkey Red Collection does show how textile designs might have been put together. This image shows a collage of fabric pieces and drawn or painted figures which the textile designer was trying out to see if they would work together. John Orr Ewing & Co., 1880s.

Paper and cotton; height 247 mm; width 300 mm

National Museums Scotland
A.1962.1266.9.5.6687

hiring designers as full-time employees, as in 1855 when Archibald Orr Ewing & Co., from their Glasgow premises in St Vincent Place, advertised:

> WANTED, a DESIGNER of first rate taste and ability practically acquainted with the working of Turkey Red Printed Goods. To a thoroughly competent party liberal encouragement will be offered. To be employed in Town.[4]

Similar advertisements appeared throughout the 1850s, although usually without naming the employer concerned, seeking designers 'accustomed to the styles for Turkey red goods to draw up patterns to order'; or, in another instance, a Turkey red drawer 'accustomed to print field work'.[5] Other advertisements of the same period, some placed by Manchester firms, were seeking experienced managers, printers, warehousemen, salesmen or buyers, and in 1861 there was a search from Manchester for 'a young man who practically understands the process of Turkey red dyeing and has a general knowledge of Chemistry'.[6] Designers in the calico printing industry migrated back-and-forth to Turkey red printing, as indicated in another advertisement. 'DESIGNER WANTED for a Calico Print works, one who has some experience in Turkey red styles would be preferred.'[7] Individuals in all of these trades also advertised themselves as available for work, including men based in Manchester who were willing to relocate to Glasgow, with contact available through Post Office boxes to preserve their anonymity.

As an aristocracy of labour, pattern designers were involved in various aspects of social life beyond the textile industry, including working men's education and the church, as is apparent from the following account of a meeting in the Vale of Leven:

> Alexandria – On Friday evening last, a number of the friends of Mr John Stewart, pattern designer, entertained him to a supper in Mr McLintock's, Alexandria, for the purpose of congratulating him on his success as an essayist on the 'Sabbath Question'; and also to testify their esteem for his amiable disposition and extensive public usefulness. Among the gentlemen present were Mr T. Schindler, chairman, Messrs Guthrie and Sharp, croupiers, Dr Connell, W. D. Clark Esq etc. Supper being concluded, the Chairman gave the usual loyal and patriotic toasts, which were responded to by the company, after which, in a felicitous and appropriate speech, he proposed Mr Stewart's health to which Mr S. replied in most becoming terms. Among other toasts the following were proposed by Messrs Turner, Richardson and D. Bell etc. 'The Vale of Leven Mechanics Institution'; 'John Henderson Esq., Park'; 'Young Men's Societies'; etc. During the evening several appropriate songs were exquisitely sung by Messrs McKellar, Mather and M. Clark, which added much to the enjoyment of the company, and the duties of mine host (it is sufficient to say), were performed in his usual style.[8]

Some Turkey red pattern designers worked in Glasgow from drawing offices alongside the salesrooms and warehouses, but pattern designers and trainees were also based in the Vale of Leven at the print works, as the quote above suggests. Progress from the Vale to Glasgow probably represented a career advance for talented individuals, and Turkey red manufacturers who advertised for designers often specified the attractions of a Glasgow-based job. But many designs for this and other cotton printing sectors were purchased from specialist textile design studios in Paris and at least one of the Dunbartonshire-born and trained pattern designers, who was listed in the *Post Office Directory* for 1861 as the employee of Henry Monteith & Co., and later became a noted landscape artist, James Docharty (1829–78), worked in Paris as a pattern designer in the mid-

1860s before returning to Glasgow to set up as a freelance designer.[9] Design training was mostly through apprenticeships, though a small design school had been founded in Edinburgh in the mid-eighteenth century and the mid-nineteenth century saw the founding of several new design schools in major industrial centres such as Glasgow and Paisley as part of a national movement for improvements in British design.[10]

The Glasgow Government School of Design, founded in 1845, was partly funded by an annual grant of £600, but most of the income in the first few years was from donations and student fees. There were 785 male students in 1853, mostly undertaking early morning or evening classes in conjunction with employment, and 183 female students, most of them described as having 'no occupation'. The majority of students of both genders were in the 15 to 26 years age category. Of the employed male students, the largest single group were 'mechanical engineers', many presumably associated with the textile industry, but textile design was also well represented with six calico printing engravers, 24 pattern designers, 53 pattern designer apprentices and 13 pattern makers. This was a group which, taken together, comprised 15 per cent of the total male employed student body and it was matched in numbers by students working as clerks and warehousemen, many doubtless also involved in the textile industry.[11]

The design school offered classes in 'designing suited to metals, wood, stone, pottery; also, to silk, wool, cotton, paper and lace'. There was instruction in painting, perspective, figure drawing, architectural drawing and modelling. The 'morning school' was from 7.00 am to 9.00 am every weekday and the evening classes were from 8.00 pm to 10.00 pm. The 'public classes' cost 2s per month and the 'private class', which ran during the day, was £1 11s 6d per quarter. Money prizes were offered annually to the best work in a number of categories, with the prize-winning entries exhibited for the public. John Buchanan (1819–98), pattern designer, botanist and botanical artist was probably one of the earliest students. Buchanan was a native of Levenside in Dunbartonshire where his father was a tenant farmer. He was educated at the local parish school and mechanics institute, and apprenticed as a pattern designer in the Vale of Leven in his early teens before moving to Glasgow to become foreman of the drawing shop of Turkey red manufacturer Henry Monteith & Co. at Barrowfield, which was particularly known for its floral designs. He developed an interest in botany, which he first studied in Dunbartonshire where there was a flourishing natural history society, and later developed with botanical drawing classes in Glasgow. After

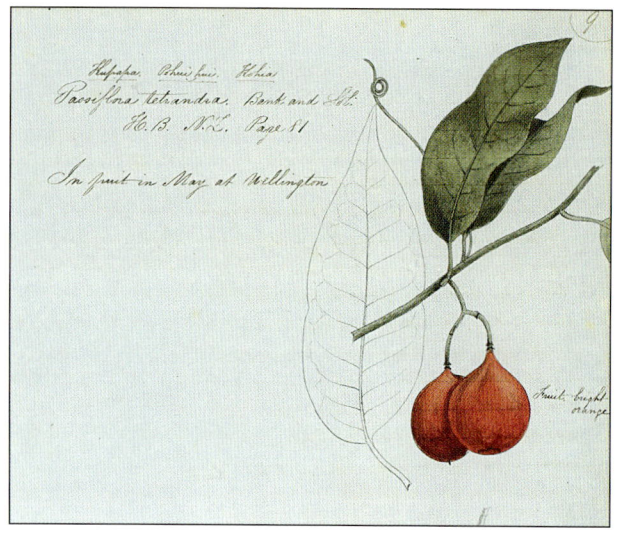

Figure 3.2

Illustration of Kohia, New Zealand passion fruit, *Passiflora tetrandra*, from page 9 of John Buchanan's notebook. Born in the Vale of Leven and a noted botanical artist, Buchanan was a Turkey red textile designer before he emigrated to New Zealand.

Auckland War Memorial Museum, NZ. MS41

emigrating to New Zealand in the early 1850s – a route taken by many ambitious young men – he made a living and reputation as a botanist and botanical artist[12] [Fig. 3.2].

Attendance at design schools was supplemented with private study in local public libraries, where students could inspect collections of design manuals, some produced in France by well-known textile designers. Trade publications such as the *Journal of Design and Manufactures* were also available and included locally produced designs, such as those of William Stirling & Sons, whose Turkey red Swiss chintz velvet featured in the edition for September 1851. Students had access to museum exhibitions of imported fine textiles, and could study such textile sample collections as that compiled by John Forbes Watson, on behalf of the government, for informing manufacturers of Indian designs[13] [Fig. 3.3].

Design schools were attractive for students, but despite the initial enthusiasm from industry there was frequent complaint that textile manufacturers were unwilling to give their employees the necessary time to attend classes and improve their skills. Manufacturers in general were also criticised for not providing schools with financial support and because they continued to favour foreign-purchased designs. 'In Manchester and Paisley the manufacturers, we are told, "do not generally recognize the elementary teaching as being of sufficient direct value to themselves to make it worth their while to support it".' This analysis highlighted the continued dependence on foreign designers and pointed to one of the ongoing problems with the students coming out of the schools:

> The distance and the interval which separate the young student from the pattern designer who can compete with the French artists is too great. Because the results are not immediate, they [the British manufacturers] deny that the school is of benefit to them.[14]

However, the article also suggested that the design schools had had an impact at entry level for young pattern designers at the start of their careers – 'At Glasgow some of the manufacturers have not employed anybody but pupils of the School of Design for 20 years, yet at Glasgow the subscriptions have fallen to nothing!' The issue rumbled on for decades as a cause for concern. In 1882, Lord Lieutenant of Dunbartonshire, Mr H. K. Crum Ewing stated, when raising a fund to found a design school in Helensburgh, that Scottish calico printers 'still have to depend largely upon Paris for the supply of their best patterns'.[15]

Evidence of the design process contained within the Museum's Turkey Red Collection, and in the Bombay Pattern Book in particular, highlight the use of in-house copying and minor alterations from existing designs, or from those produced by competitor companies and native craftsmen in the bazaars. Yet the Turkey Red Collection does include a few beautifully executed designs drawn on paper that can only have come from highly skilled artists, though whether these were British (in-house employees or freelancers) or French is unknown [Fig. 3.4]. And some of the commemorative handkerchief

Figure 3.3

A fine cotton turban sample from Jaipur, one of the hundreds of Indian textile samples distributed by John Forbes Watson in the 1860s in his *Textile Manufactures of India*, which was meant to educate and inspire British manufacturers. Similar designs appear throughout the Turkey Red Collection, 19th century. Indian School.dsa

Harris Museum and Art Gallery/The Bridgeman Art Library

Figure 3.4

This intricately drawn design for cylinder printing is not quite complete, as the paisley shapes at the edge of the pattern have not been coloured in fully. John Orr Ewing & Co., 1860s.

Paper; height 445 mm; width 385 mm

National Museums Scotland A.1962.1266.11.2211

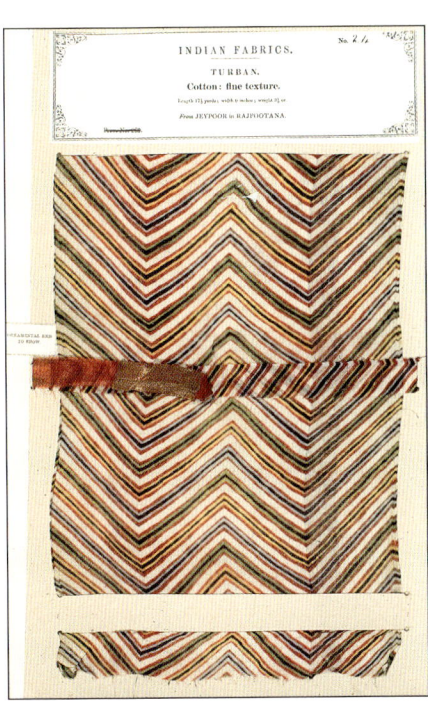

designs were original and well designed, though others relied on copying from popular magazine images. John Orr Ewing & Co. was particularly noted for good design in the 1850s and 1860s, and its fabrics appeared more frequently than those of any other firm in the pages of William Stirling & Sons' Bombay Pattern Book, with instructions to make copies for sale in India. This type of design theft drew harsh criticism, as recorded in some of the court cases that were brought to protect copyright.

> The differences found [between two designs subject to legal dispute] are just those that might be inserted by a third-rate designer in trying to take the market with a chintz as like the pursuer's as possible without making an exact copy. The alterations of the outer edge of the pine, of the turn of small end, and of the flower in the centre, the addition of a rosebud to the rose, and the introduction of horseshoes or crescents in the ground in lieu of spots are just differences such as would occur to a barren and costive brain endeavouring to avoid making an exact copy rather than to a designer of any originality.[16]

Copyright and copying

By the time the Scottish Turkey red industry reached its peak in the late nineteenth century, the copying or imitation of designs from India or Europe had been a central element of the British calico printing industry for over 200 years.[17] The early industry was London-based and mainly supplied an élite market, but these high quality craft workshops soon faced competition from northern producers, particularly in Lancashire, whose modern machines and factories produced cheaper products for a growing working-class market. By the 1780s, London calico printers complained that northern manufacturers copied their original designs, and that cheap imitations undercut their profits.[18] At a time when other areas of industrial innovation, and producers of intellectual property more generally, were crying out for legislative protection, this concern resulted in the first copyright law relating to the textile printing industry. In 1787, printed textile designs could be placed under copyright for a period of two months, as long as the name of the proprietor was visible on each piece of fabric. This protection was extended to three months in 1794.[19]

Needless-to-say, copyright for two or three months was not long enough to secure the commercial advantages of a new design, and despite the legislation, copying continued unabated. In the words of a major proponent of extended copyright protection, the celebrated calico printer, James Thomson of Clitheroe:

> It was never pretended, at that day, that the trade would be driven abroad if one portion of it was not allowed to pilfer the other: and the school of PIRATICAL-ECONOMY was not then founded, which has since arisen, building on the practice of the pirates of Manchester and Glasgow.[20]

James Thomson, born in Blackburn in 1779 of Scottish parents, was trained in the printing trade in Glasgow, where he also attended chemistry classes at the University, before working in London in the counting house of Joseph Peel & Co. He formed his own calico printing business at Primrose near Clitheroe in Lancashire in partnership with his brother, who ran the Manchester offices, and the firm rose to be one of the greatest of its day. Thomson pioneered the development of high quality textile design and was a leading supporter of the Manchester Design School in the 1840s. He wrote several pamphlets calling for extensions in copyright protection, and in doing so in an age that celebrated 'free trade', he also sought to define what was meant by the principle.

> Mr Thomson very clearly points out that Copyright in Design is the protection of property created by labour, skill and capital and should not be confounded with the idea of 'Protection to Trade' or 'Exclusive Privileges' or with 'Monopoly'; and all that he says in respect of Design is most pertinent to the rights of Invention – a subject Parliament will hear enough of next session.[21]

These last comments, from the *Journal of Design and Manufactures* in 1850, which proselytised so-called 'good design' and was edited by Henry Cole of Great Exhibition fame, came a decade after further developments in copyright legislation. The Design Act of 1839 established a central designs registry in London, where records would be kept of all designs that were invested with copyright, although protection was still only for three months and the cost of registering in or consulting the volumes was considerable. A Parliamentary Select Committee was appointed in 1840 to investigate the matter further, leading to the Design Act of 1842, with a reduced registration fee and copyright extension to nine months for printed dress fabrics and twelve months for furniture fabrics.[22] The next significant legislation was not until 1883, and although the records beginning in 1839 still exist in the collections of the National Archives

Figure 3.5

Simple, traditional patterns such as these bandanna or handkerchief designs were almost impossible to protect under copyright legislation as they would have been in long-standing use. John Orr Ewing & Co., 1860s.

Cotton and paper; height 526 mm; width 330 mm

National Museums Scotland
A.1962.1266.29.1785

at Kew, and show that many firms did register large numbers of designs as before, copying and design imitation continued and there were still problems with defining what constituted an original design and was thus worthy of copyright protection. The debate and concern was fuelled in part by the rise of the 'named designer' from the 1870s, which meant that design as intellectual property became a personal as well as commercial consideration.[23]

The Scottish Turkey red industry was still relatively new when the Design Act of 1839 introduced the first public register for copyrighted designs. Archibald Orr Ewing & Co. was the first to seek design copyright in 1848, just three years after the firm was founded, registering four patterns that year which illustrate the ambiguity of so-called 'original' design. The first was an imitation tie-dye pattern with yellow and white diamond formations and was probably intended for the emerging Indian market.[24] It is a relatively simple design, and while the following three are more visually exciting, their design components of floral patterns, imitation tie-dye and imitation ikat dyeing are similarly derived from traditional Indian motifs.[25] It is likely that such designs were worth protecting because of their long-standing popularity, since the Indian market was regarded as less susceptible to the whims of fashion than the European.[26] It is also possible that the registration of designs so soon after the firm was established was a profile-raising exercise, or an experiment, or even a mistake born out of naïve business practices. Whatever the reason, the venture into copyright was short-lived and it was 1872 before Archibald Orr Ewing & Co. sent another design for registration in London.

The next to place a design under copyright was John Orr Ewing & Co. in 1862, quickly followed by 42 more designs in the same year. Indeed, from 1862 onwards the firm submitted large numbers of designs, averaging 22 per year, with a peak of 187 registrations in 1867. The Museum's Bombay Pattern Book, maintained by William Stirling & Sons, shows a higher level of copying from John Orr Ewing &

Co.'s patterns than from any other firm, so it seems likely that the latter was seeking desperately to protect its own commercial property. In contrast, William Stirling & Sons waited until April 1874 before submitting its first patterns for copyright, consisting of three imitation tie-dye designs, which were probably intended for scarves or saris in the Indian market.

It is possible that the Vale of Leven firms were submitting designs for copyright before these dates. It is known that some English firms used an intermediary, such as a lawyer or merchant, to register designs with the Board of Trade, and Scottish manufacturers may have done the same.[27] The broad conclusion remains, however, that design registration was not considered a necessity, possibly because of the cost involved, and also because of the reliance on 'traditional' designs.

The scale of design registration by the three Vale of Leven firms between 1842 and 1883 (when a further copyright act was introduced, extending protection to five years) is indicated in Table 3.1 below. John Orr Ewing & Co. dominated, but the numbers are modest compared to other firms, such as James Thomson & Co. of Clitheroe, who in the first eight years of the 1842 Design Act submitted over 5,000 designs to the Board of Trade, the largest number from any manufacturer of the time.[28]

Table 3.1: Designs sent to the Board of Trade by Vale of Leven Turkey red manufacturers, 1842–83

Vale of Leven firm	Average number of designs sent per year	Total number of designs sent to the Board of Trade
William Stirling & Sons	4	181
John Orr Ewing & Co.	22	892
Archibald Orr Ewing & Co.	3	127

Source: BT43, Board of Trade Design Registers, the National Archives, London

All three firms sent a variety of style types to be protected by copyright and usually did so in sets of designs, which was a common strategy employed to confuse competitors as they could not be sure which design was thought by the proprietor to be the most profitable.[29] Certain trends can be discerned from these registered designs.

Figure 3.6

This intricate design was registered for copyright in April 1876. It was not until the Design Registers in the National Archives, Kew, were examined that it was known that the design, and the pattern book from which it came, belonged to John Orr Ewing & Co.

Cotton; height 401 mm; width 249 mm

National Museums Scotland
A.1962.1266.31.12.18

The 1860s, for instance, saw large numbers of peacock patterns, as well as small print or filling designs for saris, which were often described as 'Swiss prints'. Many of the peacock patterns were re-registered at later dates, suggesting their popularity and profitability. The 1870s was notable for intricately drawn, multi-coloured patterns based on stylised flowers or paisley cone motifs, a type of design made possible by new technological developments in printing [Fig. 3.6].

Of the 892 designs submitted by John Orr Ewing & Co., nearly a quarter comprise floral and foliage patterns ranging from the naturalistic to heavily stylised, almost abstract floral shapes. Over one-fifth of the submitted designs had some sort of animal or bird as the main motif of the pattern – and of these animal patterns, by far the most common was the peacock. Many of the peacock patterns first introduced in the 1860s were re-registered at a later date, suggesting that they were popular and profitable designs for the firm. Other animals included lions, elephants and tigers. One design, registered in 1874, depicts a lion holding a sabre, with a sun rising over the lion's shoulder. These were the national emblems of Iran's Qajar dynasty, which is where this fabric was probably bound [Fig. 3.7]. John Orr Ewing & Co. also registered commemorative designs, which were intended for the domestic as well as the European market, such as a handkerchief to celebrate the election of George I to the Greek throne in 1863.[30]

Figure 3.7

A design similar to this, but with floral decorations and no peacock, was registered for copyright in 1878. It was produced by John Orr Ewing & Co. using the cylinder printing technique. Late 19th century.

Cotton; height 340 mm; width 334 mm

National Museums Scotland A.1962.1266.10.5.4739

A striking feature of the 127 designs registered by Archibald Orr Ewing & Co. is the use of black colouring in their patterns, sometimes as a ground and sometimes providing the detail, a type of print that was popular at home but not in India. William Stirling & Sons, though late starters, had a clear market in mind for most of their registered designs and submitted large numbers of figurative patterns containing stylised peacocks, parrots and flowers, very similar in character to embroidered Indian fabrics of the period.[31] William Stirling & Sons also appear to have been the only Vale of Leven firm who submitted white stencil designs for copyright. These show a clear East Asian influence with motifs of bridges, pagodas, East Asian writing and fans, probably intended for sale at home to middle-class consumers with a growing interest in Japanese arts and crafts [Fig. 3.8].

As with printers in the rest of Britain, despite copyright the Vale of Leven manufacturers still engaged in design fraud amongst them-

Figure 3.8

Sample of printed cotton cloth with a white Japanese influenced stencil design of books and delicate trailing vines with green detail. Taken from a furniture fabric pattern book. Unidentified Vale of Leven firm, post-1876.

Cotton; height 505 mm; width 610 mm

National Museums Scotland A.1962.1266.21.1.4224

selves. The very first design that William Stirling & Sons submitted for copyright in 1874 – with motifs of peacocks, the tree of life and dancing girls, all made up of small mosaic-like squares giving the appearance of tie-dye – was almost identical to one submitted by John Orr Ewing & Co. just a month before, with only minor differences in the use of colours.[32] With the large number of designs submitted to the Board of Trade on a daily basis, it is not surprising that some copies slipped through the net. The close timing of these two registrations is intriguing and certainly points to foul play on the part of one, if not both, firms. A later illustration of design theft again involved the same two firms. In 1877 John Orr Ewing & Co. accused William Stirling & Sons of stealing a design. John Matheson, Stirling's principal partner, defended his firm by saying:

> It has been the Custom as long as I remember for samples of Dyeing and printing to find their way from one work to another. As a matter of fact this is a common practice amongst the Vale of Leven Works, and certainly not less so in that of Messrs John Orr Ewing and Co.'s.[33]

John Matheson's words echoed those of witnesses called before the Select Committee on Copyright of Designs over 40 years previously, when asked about design protection, and it seems that despite the legislation, copying had remained normal practice.³⁴

Protection against fraud was likewise apparent in other aspects of the Turkey red industry, such as trademark design. Vale of Leven firms made use of elaborately decorated trademark labels to identify different products or quality grades, particularly for the international market [see Figs 3.9 and 3.10]. These labels were carefully designed to appeal to consumers in whichever market the cloth was intended, and often works of art in their own right. Some had exotic animals, such as elephants or parrots; others showed local deities or figures in traditional dress. The use of pictorial trademark designs was particularly important when many of the customers in overseas markets were illiterate, or where the product was widely distributed across many cultures and languages. According to one report, customers in rural India used these labels to distinguish between heavy- and light-weight yarns – labels for heavy-weight yarns, for instance, were

Figure 3.9

The trade mark labels used by the Turkey red firms were carefully designed to appeal to different international markets. Those intended for India often used Indian religious iconography or mythology. This label was used by John Orr Ewing & Co., and shows Krishna and his wives. John Orr Ewing & Co., *c.*1880.

University of Glasgow Archive Services, United Turkey Red Co. Ltd collection, GB0248 [UGD13/7A/3/3]

Figure 3.10

Trade mark labels sometimes linked aspects of British popular culture with international customers for Turkey red cotton. In this case, Indian men are depicted on a 'joy wheel', which was a fairground attraction commonly seen in Britain. John Orr Ewing & Co., *c.*1900.

University of Glasgow Archive Services, United Turkey Red Co. Ltd collection, GB0248 [UGD13/7/A/3/10]

more heavily gilded than those used for light weights.[35] Efforts were made to limit confusion and there was a central register from the 1870s showing which firm 'owned' which trademark.[36] However, as with traditional textile designs, many well-known trademark motifs were used by a number of firms and disputes remained the norm. In 1873, for instance, in what was described in the press as an 'important trade-mark case', Archibald Orr Ewing & Co. took E. & J. Steegmann, commission merchants, to court, accusing them of taking one of their label designs and using it to promote 'third parties' yarn', to their 'injury and loss'. The court found in favour of Archibald Orr Ewing & Co., describing the goods of E. & J. Steegmann as 'of an inferior description'.[37]

Other areas of design protection included patents for machinery for printing and dyeing, which were sometimes sold to rivals to prevent design theft. In 1869, John Orr Ewing & Co. was approached by Stevenson & Mckenzie, agents acting on behalf of Henry Monteith & Co., famous for printed bandannas and one of Ewing's biggest rivals. Monteith & Co. wanted to acquire a particular design of yarn-dyeing machine, for which John Orr Ewing & Co. owned the patent. It was agreed that Monteith & Co. could erect these machines at their Blantyre works for the sum of £200 per machine – a high price. The middlemen in this delicate negotiation took a commission of almost half the fee.[38] A year later, John Orr Ewing & Co. heard of a similar dyeing machine being patented elsewhere and immediately sought to discover if it was an 'infringement' of their own.[39]

Exhibitions of Turkey red

Britain had 22 'international' exhibitions in the second half of the nineteenth century; the first, the Great Exhibition at London's Crystal Palace in 1851, acting as a model for those that followed in Europe and America and in the British colonial capitals, as well as in the main British provincial cities, starting with Manchester in 1856. The first Scottish exhibition was in Edinburgh in 1886 and there were bigger events in Glasgow in 1888, 1901 and 1911. These international exhibitions, which were many years in the planning, were held during the summer months and attracted large numbers. Glasgow in 1888 had over six million visitors from near and far and was a huge commercial success, with the profits and some of the exhibits going into the founding of the Kelvingrove Art Gallery and Museum.[40] Great exhibitions acted to showcase the cities in which they were held, and were tourist attractions. They operated commercially as vast displays of goods and services, with individual firms mounting elaborate exhibition stands to highlight their best product or patents and to attract new customers. Entrepreneurs could view competitors' products, designers could be inspired, and workers had an opportunity to see the fruits of their labour displayed to public acclaim.

Several Scottish Turkey red firms were represented at the 1851 Great Exhibition in London: these included Henry Monteith & Co., Archibald Orr Ewing & Co., and William Stirling & Sons. The latter's displays in the 'world's exhibition' section were focussed on a widely reported 'exhibition handkerchief'. Described as being of 'questionable taste' in the *Glasgow Herald*, the handkerchief or bandanna comprised a series of views of the Crystal Palace, with the figure of Britannia at the centre, surrounded by the 'usual military trophies, flags, muskets and cannon, all of which are intertwined with sprigs of laurel, for peace, and the thistle, rose and shamrock, for the Three Kingdoms'. There was a border with designs emblematic of the 'four quarters of the globe'.

> For Asia there is a recumbent figure, with a drawn scimitar, while an elephant browses off the tall trees overhead. A border of tropical plants, with a boa intertwined on one side, and a monkey clinging to the twigs on the other, finish this compartment.

A final outer border included designs representative of the means whereby the world trade in Turkey red textiles was made possible.

> Steam boats and sailing craft – railway trains with passengers and goods' trucks – for Europe and America; a caravan with loaded camels for the overland journey; and elephants etc for India.[41]

Handkerchiefs such as these (other firms produced much the same) were sold as souvenirs during the run of the exhibition and were devices for advertising the company and its design expertise.

Turkey red cotton was on prominent display not only in the 1851 exhibition courts, but also as a highly colourful furnishing fabric for the seating erected for the opening events [Fig. 3.11]. Indeed, textiles were commonly used in exhibition spaces to decorate the utilitarian temporary buildings in which they took place. This was described in the press for 1851, as preparations advanced at Crystal Palace:

> A considerable portion of the Turkey red cloth used in the lining of stalls and as a background for the gallery railings, has been placed and this, combined with the masses of brilliant colours beginning to

Figure 3.11

Turkey red fabric not only appeared as an exhibit at the 1851 Crystal Palace Exhibition, it was also used to decorate the various courts. This illustration by Joseph Nash shows the furniture court with its swathes of red cloth hanging from the balcony. Taken from plate 17, vol. II of the album, 'Dickinson's Comprehensive Pictures of the Great Exhibition of 1851, from the originals painted for Prince Albert, by Messrs. Nash, Haghe, Roberts, R. A., etc.', 1854.

© Victoria and Albert Museum, London

show all over the area of the building, tells with best effects upon the general aspect of the interior.[42]

The use of Turkey red for bunting was also popular and in evidence in Glasgow in 1888, for when the royal party, headed by Queen Victoria, travelled from the railway station for the exhibition opening, it was noted that John Orr Ewing & Co. hung Turkey red and yellow cloth in celebratory display over the front of their city centre warehouse and offices.[43]

Public displays of textiles in Britain had a history that long preceded the Great Exhibition of 1851 and there were numerous local or short-term exhibitions of Turkey red cottons along with other manufactured goods, often run as Christmas events. The Board of Trustees for the 'encouragement of Scottish manufacturers' had for decades held an annual 'exposition' in November and December, usually in Edinburgh in the Royal Institution on Princes Street. In the summer of 1842 they advertised for 'manufactures of every kind of fabric, pattern drawers, designers and others' to come forward with goods for display that were 'remarkable for superiority of fabric, novelty in the application of material, elegance of form or pattern, beauty of design and harmony of colours'.[44] These events were popular with visiting audiences, as were those in Glasgow, like the 'Grand Exhibition during the holidays [Christmas 1846] in the Glasgow City Hall'.[45] Local exhibitions were attractive to manufacturers but also to local pattern designers, many of them young apprentices who studied part time at the design schools and through successful exhibition hoped to advance their careers. As the exhibition movement became an international phenomenon, the mainly working-class public was eager to see more. Excursion trains ran from the big cities, including Glasgow, taking visitors to London for the Great Exhibition of 1851, and by the 1860s the Thomas Cook tours company were advertising 'all inclusive' working men's trips from Glasgow to Paris for the exhibition of 1867. Indeed John Christie, one of the managers with John Orr Ewing & Co. corresponded with Thomas Cook & Co. in 1878 over a proposed group trip to the Paris exhibition of that year, seeking information on first- and second-class prices.[46]

Scottish textile manufacturers had a strong presence at all of the Paris international exhibitions, and details were recorded at length in the Scottish press. This is not surprising since Paris was the centre of the European textile design industry, offering insights into developing fashions as well as the opportunity to meet with French designers and purchase new patterns [Fig. 3.12]. In 1855, which was the first of the Paris exhibitions, there was a large contingent of Glasgow exhibitors in the category of 'printed muslins and cambrics' including John Black & Co. and Henry Monteith & Co., who also produced Turkey red

Figure 3.12

This is an intricate copperplate printed design which was produced in 1855 for the Exposition Universelle in Paris, showing the front of the Palais de l'Industrie. It is not known which of the Vale of Leven firms produced this design, but a likely candidate is William Stirling & Sons, who also produced a commemorative design for the Great Exhibition at the Crystal Palace in 1851.

Cotton; height 153mm; width 175mm

National Museums Scotland
A.1962.1266.7.2.20

cottons. The firm of D. J. Macdonald & Co. of Glasgow had a highlighted display of 'Turkey red goods', and one local reporter was impressed by what he saw:

> It strikes me that our Manchester and Glasgow exhibitors have either imbibed a portion of French taste or been assisted by French artistic skills in arranging and displaying their goods: for I never saw the cotton fabrics of our country look so elegant and attractive in their general effect as they do here.[47]

Attending an international exhibition and mounting a display was an expensive undertaking for the firms concerned, so it had to have some financial rational for business development or marketing. The exhibition stand that was commissioned by William Stirling & Sons for the Manchester Royal Jubilee Exhibition of 1887, made of wood and glass, was 15 feet wide, 20 feet deep and 13 feet high, and cost £175 to make, with the cost of transport and interior decoration added to that. It was subsequently used at the 1888 Glasgow exhibition. Renting a space at the Manchester exhibition cost £50 and there were also travel and accommodation costs for those who attended the displays during the run of the event, which lasted several months.[48] William Stirling & Sons' Manchester display was particularly noted for its Turkey red lace curtains and the Turkey red and purple furnishing velvets.[49] The dismantled exhibition stand lay in one of the firm's Dunbartonshire factories for many years after these two events of the 1880s and was used again, along with another owned by John Orr Ewing & Co., for the Glasgow Exhibition of 1901.[50]

The high-point for Scottish Turkey red exhibitions in the later nineteenth century was the Glasgow International Exhibition of 1888, which was remarkable for its India displays, including a group of Indian craftsmen and shop workers at a retail stand who were also seen a few years earlier at the London India and Colonial Exhibition of 1886.[51] The India displays were organized by John Muir, a frequent visitor to India, who was sole proprietor in the Glasgow firm of James Findlay & Co., manufacturers of cotton since the mid-eighteenth century, who also had interests in the tea trade and in jute manufacture in India.[52] There was an extensive 'Indian Pavilion' mounted by Doulton & Co., the London-based manufacturer of pottery and household ceramics, which housed potters making hand-thrown commemorative wares[53] [Fig. 3.13]. India themes were also evident in the refreshments provision, including curry houses and tearooms.[54]

Not surprisingly, the Turkey red manufacturers emphasised Indian themes, reflecting the importance of this market. The stand occupied by F. Steiner & Co. of Manchester included several full-size figures or mannequins of Indian women in glass cases, showing colourful fabrics against dark skins and jewellery. The same was seen in Archibald Orr Ewing & Co.'s display, generating the following newspaper report:

> While the gaudy lines of these [textiles] find only limited favours under our cloudy skies, it is in the Oriental countries, and in contrast with dark skin, that their full value is appreciated. The firm have, therefore, done well in showing at one end of their stand a figure of an Indian female dressed completely in their fabrics. The figure stands holding a basket on the head and is complete even to the gold bangles, anklets, necklet and earrings. No one can fail to see with what effect the warm and glowing colours of the Turkey red fabric tell in contrast with swarthy skin of the oriental.[55]

Figure 3.13

India was a prominent theme at the Glasgow International Exhibition of 1888. This view of the Central Hall shows the terracotta Indian Pavilion which was created by Doulton & Co. The products of both Archibald Orr Ewing & Co. and John Orr Ewing & Co. received mentions in press reports of the exhibition.

© CSG CIC Glasgow Museums and Libraries Collection: The Mitchell Library, Special Collections

But the content of the exhibition cases also included other types of goods, with John Orr Ewing & Co. giving prominence to 'a mat or table cover displayed in a special case [which] shows on a Turkey red ground the Royal arms and the Glasgow arms in colours'. This was described as an 'exhibition piece designed to demonstrate the purity and brilliance of the colours of the firm'. There were 'delicate pinks up to the full and deep reds' displayed in a spectrum. There were 'one or two samples in which a peculiar combination of reds and greens on a fine textured cotton gives an appearance which on hasty glance might be taken for that of silk'. Whereas 'in other portions of the stand cotton velvets of fine colour are placed, and the damask-looking textures in two tints of red very fairly resemble the richer materials they simulate'.[56] However, one reviewer, though full of praise for what he saw displayed behind glass, wanted to touch the fabrics too:

> It may well be remarked ... that a useful aid to the technical examiner would be a bunch of patterns hung outside for handling if

desired, as has been done in a neighbouring court. It is of importance to note the relative softness of feel of the several dyes of the different makers; and although as a general rule there is not much to pick and choose between our several dyers in this respect, yet it would be a satisfaction to many to examine and compare materials.[57]

The formation of the United Turkey Red Co. Ltd in 1898 reduced competition within the industry, but did not diminish enthusiasm for mounting exhibitions of Turkey red goods, particularly in Glasgow. Despite concerns about failing markets, the UTR Board requested 48 square feet of floor space for their exhibit at the Glasgow International Exhibition of 1901. They debated at length on the subject of the display cabinets, what they should include and how they should be labelled, determined to preserve the original names of the three firms involved, although these had been disbanded on the formation of UTR. The board finally agreed to exhibit 'a whole range of coloured yarns in bundles and packets, including specimens of mercerised yarns', which reflected the main orientation of the business by this stage in its history. But fabrics were also on display, including plain reds, twills and velvets, prints, chintzes, 'two reds', sari dresses and many more.[58]

Notes

1. National Museums Scotland: Turkey Red Collection. Accession no. A.1962.1266.31.6.
2. UGA: UGD13/4/4. Wage book, 1845.
3. *Who's Who in Glasgow in 1909* (Glasgow, 1909).
4. *Glasgow Herald*, 19 January 1855.
5. *Glasgow Herald*, 5 February and 22 March 1859.
6. *Glasgow Herald*, 26 August 1861.
7. *Glasgow Herald*, 21 December 1863.
8. *Glasgow Herald*, 6 October 1849.
9. *Dundee Courier and Argus*, 8 April 1878.
10. Lara Kriegel, *Grand Designs: Labor, Empire, and the Museum in Victorian Culture* (London, 2007).
11. *Glasgow Herald*, 25 April 1853.
12. *Glasgow Herald*, 5 December 1898; N. M. Adams, 'Buchanan, John: Biography', *Dictionary of New Zealand Biography*. [Accessed online 25/03/2013.]
13. F. Driver and S. Ashmore, 'The mobile museum. Collecting and circulating Indian textiles in Victorian Britain', *Victorian Studies* 52:3 (2010), pp. 353–84.
14. *Birmingham Daily Post*, 17 October 1864.
15. *Glasgow Herald*, 20 April 1882.
16. *Glasgow Herald*, 5 April 1899.
17. Kriegel, *Grand Designs*, pp. 55–56.
18. Ada K. Longfield, 'William Kilburn and the earliest copyright acts for cotton printing designs', *The Burlington Magazine*, 95:604 (1953), pp. 230–33, p. 230.
19. See David Greysmith, 'Patterns, piracy and protection in the textile printing industry', *Textile History*, 14:2 (1983), pp.165–94.
20. *Journal of Design and Manufactures* (November 1850), pp. 65–72.
21. Ibid.
22. Greysmith, 'Patterns, piracy and protection', p. 170, p. 175.
23. John Styles, 'Victorian Britain, 1837–1901', in

Michael Snodin and John Styles (eds), *Design and the Decorative Arts, Britain 1500–1900* (London, 2001), p. 390.
24 National Archives, Kew [hereafter TNA]: BT44/19 Register 1847–48, and BT43/229 registered design number 51357.
25 TNA: BT44/19 Register 1847–48 and BT43/229 registered design numbers 51808–51810.
26 Agnes M. M. Lyons, 'The textile fabrics of India and Huddersfield cloth industry', *Textile History*, 27:2 (1996), pp. 172–94, p.182.
27 Greysmith, 'Patterns, piracy and protection', p. 181.
28 S. D. Chapman, 'Quantity versus quality in the British industrial revolution: the case of printed textiles', *Northern History*, 21 (1985), pp.175–92, p. 186.
29 Philip Sykas, *The Secret Life of Textiles: Six Pattern Book Archives in North West England* (Bolton, 2005), p. 70.
30 TNA: BT44/22 Register 1861–63 and BT43/289 registered design number 166301.
31 There are surviving examples in the Victoria and Albert Museum with almost identical motifs.
32 TNA: BT44/22 Register 1861–63 and BT43/289 registered design number 166301.
33 UGA: UGD13/5/13/1/1. Memorandum of complaint. Glasgow 19 July 1877.
34 See *Report from the Select Committee on Copyright of Designs Together with the Minutes of Evidence Taken Before Them* (London, 1840).
35 *Glasgow Herald*, 5 March 1879.
36 D. M. Higgins and Geoffrey Tweedale, 'The trade marks question and the Lancashire cotton textile industry, 1870–1914', *Textile History*, 27:2 (1996), pp. 207–28, p. 210.
37 *Glasgow Herald*, 2 August 1873.
38 UGA: UGD 13/1/8/12. Letter dated 30 March 1869.
39 UGA: UGD 13/1/8/69. Letter dated 15 July 1870.
40 P. Kinchin and J. Kinchin, *Glasgow's Great Exhibitions: 1888, 1901, 1911, 1938, 1988* (Wendlebury, n.d).
41 *Glasgow Herald*, 21 February 1851.
42 *Scotsman*, 30 April 1851.
43 *Glasgow Herald*, 9 May 1888.
44 *Scotsman*, 30 July 1842.
45 *Glasgow Herald*, 21 December 1846.
46 UGA: UGD 13/1/3/358. Letter dated 1 June 1878.
47 *Scotsman*, 4 August 1855.
48 UGA: UGD 13/5/13/6/7. Letter dated 6 June 1887.
49 *Glasgow Herald*, 16 May 1887.
50 MCRO: UTR Minute Book no. 2, 2 October 1900.
51 See, Stana Nenadic, 'Exhibiting India in nineteenth-century Scotland and the impact on commerce, industry and design', *Journal of Scottish Historical Studies* (2014 forthcoming).
52 *Oxford Dictionary of National Biography Online*.
53 *Supplement to the North British Daily Mail*, 24 May 1888.
54 Kinchin and Kinchin, *Glasgow's Exhibitions*, p. 46.
55 *Supplement to the North British Daily Mail*, 26 September 1888.
56 *Supplement to the North British Daily Mail*, 25 October 1888.
57 *Glasgow Herald*, 24 May 1888.
58 MCRO: UTR Minute Book, 6 December 1899, 9 May, 6 September, 12 September and 2 October 1900, 20 February and 13 March 1901.

CHAPTER FOUR

Styles and patterns

THE NINETEENTH century saw many debates on what constituted 'good design' and there were numerous initiatives to correct what was widely regarded as 'deficiencies' in taste in Britain, particularly when compared with France. The great exhibition movement from the mid-nineteenth century spearheaded a mission to highlight and reward good design alongside technical innovation, with cultural purists such as Owen Jones or Henry Cole, also editor of the *Journal of Design and Manufactures*, loudly critical of the British printed cotton textile industry and eager to educate manufacturers in the principles of pure design through creating museum collections and publishing design manuals.[1] The Paris Universal Exhibition of 1867 marked the greatest moment of despair, as the *Edinburgh Review* reported:

> In Cotton Goods, the English display sank into insignificance by the side of the splendid show made by the French cotton trades, which greatly exceeded ours in fullness of representation and in excellence of arrangement … the muslin and lighter prints decidedly surpassed anything of the same kind produced in England, perhaps because we have not given our thoughts to such gay, fanciful and changeful elegancies.[2]

Scotland's Turkey red manufacturers were part of these debates, at least at a superficial level, having participated in several great exhibitions, including the Paris Exhibition of 1867, and submitted some of their designs for inclusion in the *Journal of Design and Manufactures* during its short existence from 1849 until 1852.[3] But the Turkey red industry was market led, not design led, and its output, though commanding an important and profitable niche in printed cottons, was 'cheap and cheerful', not luxurious. Moreover, design information from key international markets, which were often traditional and conservative in taste, was more important than aesthetically correct design manuals.

Opposite page:

Peacocks and paisley motifs are used as the border for a multi-coloured steam train (see Fig. 4.43).

National Museums Scotland

But if design debates and initiatives had only a limited impact on Scottish Turkey red manufacture, design was still an important consideration with different overseas markets demanding widely differing patterns. Developments in print technologies also had an impact, with the complexity of a pattern largely a product of the printing method that was used, which then had cost implications. Lead plate printing, for instance, tended to produce bold and relatively simple patterns since lead could not be engraved with fine lines. In some cases lead plate printed fabrics were overprinted with copper plate to produce a more intricate design, but this increased the cost. Hand block printing, the usual technique among Indian craftsmen, could produce fine and intricate patterns when hard woods were used, but the quality depended on the skill of the block cutter and some woods could not support complex designs. The repeat of a hand block printed design was also limited by size, since the block had to be relatively small for the printer to lift. Modern cylinder printing generally produced the most intricate designs, with the roller plates mainly made of copper and with new technologies allowing the introduction of multiple colours on a single print run. Such innovations were reflected in the development of highly stylised, multi-coloured semi-floral designs with elongated and intertwined leaves, which were popular among the Turkey red manufacturers in the 1870s.

Designs and patterns were determined by the eventual use of the fabric. Indian saris, for instance, were divided into three parts; a thin border which ran the length of the cloth, a field or filling area of a small, repeated pattern, and a showy end piece of large motifs, which was the part of the sari most often on view since it was draped over the shoulder or arm. Turbans, however, which were twisted and wrapped around the head, tended to have striped or zigzag patterns, which showed to good effect. Some of the main design themes are examined here, with illustrations selected from the over 40,000 textile samples that form the National Museums Scotland's Turkey Red Collection. Whether these designs represented good or bad taste is largely irrelevant. What was important for the Vale of Leven manufacturers was whether or not they sold and made a profit.

Flowers and leaves

Floral and foliate designs have a long history in printed, woven and embroidered textiles. Traditional crewelwork embroideries often included 'fanciful plant forms and trees', which provided some of the inspiration for the chintzes imported from India in the eighteenth century.[4] British printed cottons of the same period were typically of delicate floral sprigs, usually on a white ground emulating fine patterned muslins from India.[5] Textile designers were frequently trained in botanical drawing, and at least one Scottish Turkey red designer, John Buchanan, who later emigrated to New Zealand, became a celebrated botanical artist.[6] Moreover, the 'language of flowers', which gave symbolic meaning to different species of bloom and was particularly popular among the Victorians and can be seen in sentimental poetry and art, helped to shape a popular sensitivity to floral motifs that is largely lost today.[7] Most ancient cultures, including those that influenced Europe, had messages, myths and folklore attached to flowers and plants, which meant that British textile printers who exported to these markets incorporated a hybrid of cultural influences into their designs, though whether the designers or operatives were aware of the meanings is unclear.

During the mid-nineteenth century, there was a strong stress on accurate and detailed floral representation in textile design for the home market, and this naturalism, which incorporated some of the exotic blooms that could now be viewed in public botanical gardens, was aided by innovations in fine printing technologies.[8] Floral and foliate patterns for the Indian market, however, were more stylised because they were copied from traditional symbols and motifs, which often had ancient roots that can be traced in archaeology or architecture.[9] Groups of flowers were used to represent the female form, with lotus or jasmine seen as symbols of fertility. The lotus, which features in both Buddhist and Hindu culture, appears in numerous designs and in a variety of styles in the Museum's Turkey Red Collection. It was widely regarded as a symbol of divine birth, representing fertility and prosperity, as well as the spiritual power and authority of powerful deities, and was a particularly important design motif in textiles worn by women. Full and half lotus flowers appear regularly in border designs for saris, and also in the end pieces [Fig. 4.1]. The stylised lotus was commonly placed alongside a pair of parrots, which represented love, with pink the dominant colour. The most striking representation of a lotus, this time in blue, appears in a design produced by John Orr Ewing & Co. in the early 1880s, showing a part-opened flower in the hand of Lakshmi, the Hindu goddess of wealth, fertility and wisdom [Fig. 4.2].

Other floral and foliate designs without specific religious connotations were still connected with ancient traditions. Creeping or trailing vines, a motif that has been used in many cultures, appear frequently throughout the Museum's collection, sometimes stylised and almost abstract, and sometimes naturalistic. In the Indian context, a creeping

Figure 4.1 (left)

A cylinder printed pattern with stylised lotus flowers and parrots in the border and larger stylised lotus flowers in the filling. John Orr Ewing & Co., 1880s.

Cotton; height 125mm; width 260mm

National Museums Scotland
A.1962.1266.9.5.6639

Figure 4.2 (above)

Lakshmi is the Hindu goddess of wealth, fertility and wisdom. She is often depicted holding a gold pot and a blue lotus flower, as seen here. This design was produced by John Orr Ewing & Co. and placed under copyright in 1881.

Cotton; height 120mm; width 260mm

National Museums Scotland
A.1962.1266.10.5.5426

Figure 4.3

The trailing vine in this design is used as a ground and was probably produced by a discharge process. The green, yellow and white detail was then overprinted by cylinder. John Orr Ewing & Co., late 19th century.

Cotton; height 126mm; width 252mm

National Museums Scotland
A.1962.1266.10.8.7546

Figure 4.4

Many different styles of flowers were produced for the British market. This stylised pattern of a trailing vine could be purchased in one of three different colour ways. Unidentified Vale of Leven firm, *c.*1890.

Cotton; height 192mm; width 90mm

National Museums Scotland
A.1962.1266.10.1.39

vine was a common architectural motif on Hindu temples, signifying welcome or to ward off evil spirits.[10] The trailing vine could be the main component of a design (such as a filling pattern for saris) or they were used as a ground to other decorative motifs such as larger floral sprigs. The trailing vine was also popular on printed textiles for the British market, sometimes naturalistic, or with rococo flourishes to abstract leaves with jagged and angular edges, or represented in trellis formations [Figs. 4.3 and 4.4].

British furniture prints of the later nineteenth century, doubtless influenced by the work of famous designers such as William Morris, included easily recognized native flora, such as oak leaves and ferns, sometimes incorporating woodland birds. Roses were commonly placed in Turkey red designs for the home market [Fig. 4.5], as were native blooms like the primrose, the harbinger of spring and first love, which appear prominently in a design of the later 1850s commemorating successes in the Crimean War [Fig. 4.6]. Designs intended for, or influenced by, China included chrysanthemums and peonies, the former signifying good luck and the latter symbolic of nobility and

---

Figure 4.5

Floral patterns intended for the British market were often used as furnishing fabrics and tended to be printed on thicker cotton cloth. This design is from a pattern book containing two red and coloured furnishing fabric designs from the second half of the 19th century. Unidentified Vale of Leven firm, late 19th century.

Cotton; height 495 mm; width 615 mm

National Museums Scotland A.1962.1266.21.1.B1825

Figure 4.6

Primroses and leaves create decorative borders for the various vignettes of this copperplate printed design which is assumed to be connected with the Crimean War. Unidentified Vale of Leven firm, mid- to late 19th century.

Cotton; height 162 mm; width 174 mm

National Museums Scotland A.1962.1266.7.2.56

Figure 4.7 (above)

The lead plate discharge printing process was particularly suitable for producing the large, bold patterns favoured by the South Pacific islands. This design was probably intended as a sarong or pareo and is thought to have been produced by John Orr Ewing & Co. at the end of the 19th century.

Cotton; height 457mm; width 571mm

National Museums Scotland A.1962.1266.12.11.1432

Figure 4.8 (right)

Laurel wreaths, roses, oak leaves, clover leaves and various stylised flowers are used to embellish this patriotic design created for Queen Victoria's Golden Jubilee in 1887. William Stirling & Sons, 1887.

Paper; height 455mm; width 402mm

National Museums Scotland A.1962.1266.28.1.2413

peace. Other more tropical flowers such as jasmine, symbol of love, modesty and attachment, were favoured in Indonesia and in the South Pacific. In the latter, however, the taste was for large designs for use as sarongs or pareos, heavily stylised and produced using lead plate discharge printing, generally with a single colour such as white or yellow on a red ground[11] [Fig. 4.7]. Designed to appeal to the nations of the British Empire, a multi-coloured design on paper of 1887, probably for William Stirling & Sons in celebration of the Queen's Golden Jubilee, incorporated circlets of laurel leaves with roses, berries, oak leaves, clover leaves and lotus blossom, along with various other stylised blooms [Fig. 4.8].

The final design motif which can be categorised as floral is the paisley teardrop shape, which is ubiquitous throughout the Museum's Turkey Red Collection, is instantly recognized and appears in numerous forms across the globe. It is generally known as the 'paisley' through the association with the town of Paisley and the nineteenth-century Paisley shawl industry. However, what we now recognise as the paisley shape developed out of earlier patterns, although the exact evolutionary route is a matter for debate. It has been argued, for instance, that it originated in ancient Babylon and is based on a palm frond; or in ancient Persia on a pine cone. By the eighteenth century it had long been used in Indian decorative art, often called *buta* (or *boteh*) or flower, further hinting at its origins. Others liken the shape to the mango, which is used in areas of rural India as a symbol for fertility.[12] The elongated and swirling shape that we recognise today became popular in Europe in the eighteenth century with the rising demand among fashionable élites for luxurious Kashmir shawls, which were then woven more cheaply in towns like Norwich and Paisley.[13] The paisley motif appears in different forms and styles in the Turkey red prints, appealing to many markets abroad and at home. It appears both as the main decorative motif, as on a sari end piece, as well as adorning other patterns [Fig. 4.9]. It frequently appeared as small prints for filling patterns and was often used in conjunction with peacocks for the Indian market, thus combining two traditional decorative forms. Printed Turkey red shawls with paisley patterns were made for home and export to markets like Australia or North America. One beautifully drawn design on paper, which may have been intended for the Far East market, shows a paisley shape incorporating carp in a fishpond [Fig. 4.10]. Another design unites the paisley pattern with laurel leaves and Prince of Wales feathers and crown [Fig. 4.11].

Figure 4.9

Many of the paisley shapes in the Turkey Red Collection are what we would consider the 'traditional' form of a tear drop shape. This particular design was for the end-piece of a sari or shawl. The filling pattern of the fabric would consist of the small checked fabric which can be seen at the top of the sample. Archibald Orr Ewing & Co., 1880.

Cotton; height 462 mm; width 211 mm

National Museums Scotland
A.1962.1266.8.1.363

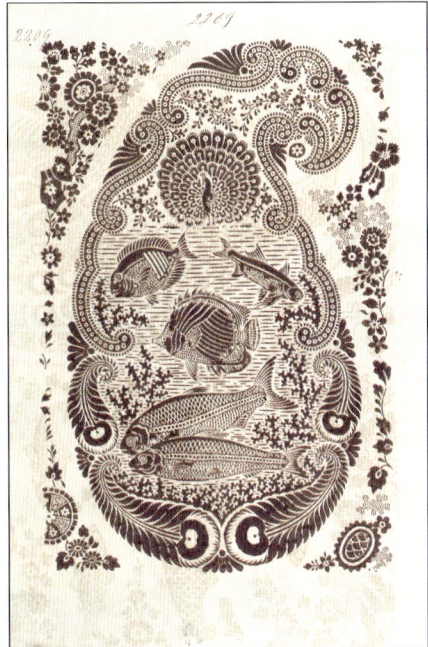

Figure 4.10

This strike off consists of a paisley motif which contains fish, scroll shapes and a peacock. It was produced by John Orr Ewing & Co. which copyrighted a very similar design in 1862, the only difference being that instead of a peacock there was a flying fish at the top of the paisley motif. John Orr Ewing & Co., c.1860.

Paper; height 385 mm; width 265 mm

National Museums Scotland
A.1962.1266.4.5.2209

73

Figure 4.11

The paisley motif was familiar to British consumers due to the popularity of paisley shawls from the late 18th century. Designs increasingly incorporated the paisley motif with British decorative symbols, as seen in this pattern which incorporates intricate stylised foliage, paisley shapes and Prince of Wales feathers. This design was drawn in 1867, possibly to commemorate the birth of Princess Louise, third child and eldest daughter to the Prince of Wales. John Orr Ewing & Co., 1867.

Paper; height 270mm; width 263mm

National Museums Scotland
A.1962.1266.11.2585

Animals and birds

Animals and birds were not so popular as floral motifs in printed textiles for clothing in Britain in the eighteenth and nineteenth centuries, though there is a rare Scottish surviving design by David Allan, showing a border that includes dove-like birds.[14] The arts and crafts movement in the later nineteenth century, through designers like William Morris or retailers like Liberty & Co., introduced more of such motifs in domestic furnishing fabrics, and this influence can be seen in the Museum's Turkey Red Collection. Animals and birds were clearly more important in other cultures, where they were frequently viewed through the lens of religion, or of myth and superstition. Aesthetically also, animals and birds in eastern and tropical countries were more exotic and spectacular than those of Europe, and therefore more likely to be included in colourful designs.

Turkey red designs for the Indian market incorporated numerous animals and birds, often reflecting the use of animals to represent Hindu deities, the most important being Ganesh, the elephant, who signifies wisdom and the removal of obstacles and was depicted in a variety of forms. Indeed, so important and distinct was the elephant that it was commonly viewed from outside as the symbol of India as a whole, and Turkey red exports to the Indian sub-continent were identified with complex highly-coloured labels which often included an elephant and, as is discussed elsewhere, were the subject of many trade disputes [Fig. 4.12]. The celebration of elephants also resided in the fact that they were an important form of transport in Asia; indeed Turkey red commemorative handkerchiefs, such as William Stirling & Sons' famous 'exhibition' handkerchief of 1851, included elephants along with loaded camels, steam trains and sailing ships, all designed to represent the trade of empire.[15] The Museum's Turkey Red Collection includes a fine design on paper, which may have been intended for a trademark rather than a textile pattern, depicting a richly-clothed elephant carrying a palanquin and a nobleman on top, with an escort of horsemen, led by a flag-bearer [Fig. 4.13].

The bird appearing most often in the Turkey Red Collection is the peacock, which represented war and immortality through its association with the Indian god Kumara, and is also connected with fertility

Figure 4.12

The trademarks used by the Turkey red firms were often as intricately designed as the printed textiles. John Orr Ewing & Co., 1867.

Cotton; height 178 mm; width 136 mm

National Museums Scotland A.1962.1266.11.234

Figure 4.13

The Turkey Red Collection contains a number of finely drawn designs intended for use in textiles or as manufacturers' labels. There is no evidence that this one, with its strange proportions, ever entered production. Unidentified Vale of Leven firm, second half of 19th century.

Paper; height 538 mm; width 340 mm

National Museums Scotland A.1962.1266.27.2

and love.[16] The peacock took many forms, with the exotic colouring and tail feathers of the male making it particularly popular for the large motif on sari end pieces [Fig. 4.14]. They were often depicted in pairs – one with its tail in full display, the other taking a more demure pose with its tail down – and came in a variety of forms, including the highly stylised and simplified, which the Scottish manufacturers faithfully copied from earlier Indian embroidered textiles. They were also portrayed in the imitation tie-dye style, with tiny mosaic-like squares used to create the outline of the bird [Fig. 4.15]. There are a number of designs in the Turkey Red Collection that represent the peacock's tail feathers alone, which are often intertwined with multi-coloured flowers. These were probably intended for the British market rather than India, and reflect a late nineteenth-century engagement with furnishing styles made popular by the European Aesthetic movement[17] [Fig. 4.16]. Of course, the importance of peacocks in Britain was also seen in the significant use of real feathers in domestic interior decoration, and in clothing for ladies hats or fans. Live peacocks were also a common sight in municipal parks and large private gardens by the end of the nineteenth century.

Parrots also appear frequently in the collection, but unlike the peacock they were rarely the main design element [Fig. 4.17]. Parrots have associations with courtship and love and are sometimes seen as messengers for lovers, which would explain why they are generally depicted as pairs. Parrots, like all flying creatures, were also linked with freedom, heaven and infinity. Several Indian goddesses are represented in art and sculpture with parrots on their hands, and this motif occurs in some of the Turkey red prints. The most common form of the parrot in the Museum's collection is highly simplified and almost cartoon-like, sometimes in multiple repeat border patterns [4.18]. The Museum's Bombay Pattern Book of the 1860s suggests that the depiction of parrots was especially common in textiles sold in western India, where the Hindu religion prevailed. Other markets with a mainly Muslim focus, where the representation of animals was religiously problematical, including Indonesia, tended to avoid recognizable figurative designs such as the parrot. One animal of great symbolic importance in Hindu culture, the cow, makes few appearances in Turkey red textile designs,

Figure 4.14

Multi-coloured peacocks surrounded by flowers are a common motif in the Turkey Red Collection. This example was produced by hand blocks. The label on this design notes that it was made void or turned off on the 25 November 1867. Unidentified Vale of Leven firm, mid-19th century.

Cotton; height 374mm; width 304mm

National Museums Scotland A.1962.1266.31.9.182

Figure 4.18 (above)

Parrots figure frequently in the borders of printed textile designs in the Turkey Red Collection, often in the simplified form that is seen here. John Orr Ewing & Co., 1880s.

Cotton; height 137 mm; width 300 mm

National Museums Scotland
A.1962.1266.10.7.6676

Figure 4.15 (above, left)

The mosaic-like appearance of this pattern is designed to imitate traditional Indian tie-dyeing, but using efficient cylinders or wood blocks rather than labour intensive hand technique, which involved small pieces of string tied around patches of fabric to prevent the dye-stuff reaching the fibre. An unidentified Vale of Leven firm, second half of 19th century.

Cotton; height 485 mm; width 315 mm

National Museums Scotland
A.1962.1266.14.2.17

Figure 4.16 (above, right)

Some designs were intended for the British or European markets, such as this one which was influenced by the Aesthetic movement. Design painted onto paper. John Orr Ewing & Co., late 19th century.

Paper; height 246 mm; width 280 mm

National Museums Scotland
A.1962.1266.6.15.2841

Figure 4.17 (below, right)

The small squares and mosaic-like effect of this design are used to imitate traditional tie-dye technique. Yellow parrots alternate with paisley motifs. This design would probably have been used as a filling pattern, perhaps for a sari or scarf. Unidentified Vale of Leven firm, late 19th century.

Cotton; height 208 mm; width 270 mm

National Museums Scotland
A.1962.1266.10.1.43

though, as anyone who has visited India will know, cows are often decorated with colour and garlands of flowers for religious festivals and celebrations. The absence of cows may have been for aesthetic reasons, since they do not have the colour or graceful form of the birds that were used to decorate women's textiles. But there may be other reasons also, such as the link with women's labour and haulage. Indeed, one design on paper, which was rejected as 'unsuitable' for the Indian market, shows cows being milked by women, alongside dancing girls, male cowherds and peacocks [Fig. 4.19].

Animals and birds were common motifs in Chinese and Japanese textiles, which had long featured in élite European households as high quality imported silks and embroidery.[18] Fashionable British designers

Figure 4.19

Not all designs were successful. This one was sent to India by William Stirling & Sons for market testing, and their agents returned it with the comment 'unsuitable'. There is no evidence that it was ever put into production. William Stirling & Sons, 1859.

Paper; height 540 mm; width 330 mm

National Museums Scotland A.1962.1266.31.6.P50

who catered for this same market, such as Christopher Dresser, incorporated such designs into their work.[19] The Scottish Turkey red manufacturers also adopted East Asian motifs for the home market and for sale abroad, including butterflies and birds such as sparrows and cranes, the latter associated with longevity, immortality and royalty in China[20] [Fig. 4.20]. Mythical creatures such as dragons also featured prominently in China-inspired designs, with one example from 1888 comprising two, three-clawed dragons and two golden pheasants, placed in a central motif surrounded by stylised butterflies on a red ground [Fig. 4.21]. All of these emblems were commonly found in imported oriental textiles: the dragon symbolic of the imperial court and government officials, the butterfly signalling joy and the golden pheasant representing beauty and fortune.[21] Among the Japan-influenced designs there were exotic fish such as the carp, butterflies, cockerels (that signified valour) and swallows, which herald good luck.

Animals were sometimes used to represent national identity. One of the most distinct designs in the Museum's collection features a lion holding a sword in its left paw, with a sun rising over its shoulder [Fig 3.7]. These were symbols of the nineteenth-century Iranian Qajar dynasty and such a design was destined for this expanding market alone. Interestingly, though red is present in prints for Iran, it is not the dominant colour, which is unusual for an industry whose reputation was built upon the production of bright, fast red. The reason reflected the demands of the market, which saw red reserved exclusively for royalty.[22] Other designs also intended for sale in the Middle East or Turkey included camels. The eagle, which appears in

Figure 4.20 (above)

Cranes were associated with longevity and royalty in China. This design also incorporates stylised lotus flowers. A similar design produced at the same time had dragons instead of cranes. John Orr Ewing & Co., late 19th century.

Cotton; height 126 mm; width 252 mm

National Museums Scotland A.1962.1266.10.8.7461

Figure 4.21 (below)

This painted design only shows a portion of what would have been the finished product. It is likely that the central motif with dragons and pheasants would have been surrounded by the ground of stylised butterflies and flowers. It is from a pattern book which is thought to have been used by William Stirling & Sons, *c.*1888.

Paper; height 460 mm; width 449 mm

National Museums Scotland A.1962.1266.28.1.2657

formal iconography in Europe and the Americas, is another animal that is used to represent national identity. A pattern that probably dates from the 1880s of an eagle in flight, holding a serpent wrapped round a stick was seemingly intended for Mexico, where the eagle and snake had been symbols of the nation since the days of the Aztecs [Fig. 4.22] The Mexican flag today still uses the same iconography.[23] Another design, this time for European sale, shows an eagle with spread wings holding lightning bolts in its talons [Fig. 4.23]. This undated pattern, which was possibly made in the 1850s to coincide with the first of the Paris International Exhibitions, was probably intended for the French market as this motif featured in the coat of arms of the Second French Empire under Napoleon III.

Crocodiles, deer, leopards, giraffes, monkeys and turkeys – the list of exotic animals that appear in Turkey red patterns is enormous [Figs. 4.24 to 4.27]. Then there are handkerchief patterns, mainly intended for home consumption or export to Europe and North America. Domestic dogs were also a common handkerchief motif, which in one

Figure 4.22

It is not known for certain if this design was intended for the Mexican market, but the eagle grasping a serpent is a motif used in the Mexican flag even to the present day, making it a likely destination. The design was hand block printed. Unidentified Vale of Leven firm, late 19th century.

Cotton; height 147 mm; width 140 mm

National Museums Scotland A.1962.1266.6.19.4

Figure 4.23

While there are many British patriotic designs in the Turkey Red Collection, other European nations were also catered to. It is thought that this design was meant for the French market, as the eagle holding lightning bolts was used in the coat of arms of the Second French Empire under Napoleon III. Unidentified Vale of Leven firm, mid-19th century.

Cotton; height 539 mm; width 598 mm

National Museums Scotland A.1962.1266.26.2.3314

Figure 4.24

Part of a series of designs which included representations of animals such as roosters; this one painted on paper is undated, but is thought to have been created at the end of the 19th century. It was probably intended for a handkerchief or shawl. Possibly produced by William Stirling & Sons, late 19th century.

Paper; height 550 mm; width 420 mm

National Museums Scotland A.1962.1266.28.2

Figure 4.25

Only a small proportion of the pattern books have been positively identified as belonging to Archibald Orr Ewing & Co., but those which have contain some interesting and intriguing designs. This hand block printed design with peacocks, giraffes and leopards was probably meant for the British or European market. Archibald Orr Ewing & Co., 1870–90.

Cotton; height 147 mm; width 140 mm

National Museums Scotland A.1962.1266.31.9.182

Figure 4.26

The name 'Turkey red' refers to the origins of the dye process, which was thought to have come from the Levant region. There is, however, one single design in the Turkey Red Collection which depicts the bird turkey. This is a two red design overprinted with white detail and it might have been meant for the North American market. It was possibly produced by Archibald Orr Ewing & Co. and dates from the 1880s.

Cotton; height 147 mm; width 140 mm

National Museums Scotland A.1962.1266.20.4.934

Figure 4.27

While the majority of the Turkey Red Collection is fabric samples, some of the designs are painted on paper, showing an earlier stage in the manufacturing and production process. The multi-coloured deer and fawns here are of a similar style to other animal designs, including a camel and a lion, and they may have been a series. Probably William Stirling & Sons, 1892.

Paper; height 372 mm; width 266 mm

National Museums Scotland A.1962.1266.28.2

Figure 4.28

Images of dogs, horses and country scenes were common in designs intended for the British market. This handkerchief was produced in the 1860s and 1870s. The design could either have a pattern in the filling, with small dogs' heads in profile, or it could be plain red with the dogs' heads in the border. John Orr Ewing & Co., 1860s–70s.

Cotton; height 147 mm; width 135 mm

National Museums Scotland
A.1962.1266.25.1016

design takes the form of a mischievous looking terrier, similar in character to Greyfriars Bobby, a popular subject from the 1860s, or the terrier depicted in the famous and much-reproduced Landseer painting *Dignity and Impudence*, which may have been copied for the design by John Orr Ewing & Co. [Fig. 4.28]. Other handkerchiefs include hunting scenes, or scenes which depicted fights between man and beast, which again may have been copied from magazines, such as the mass-circulation illustrated 'boy's-own' adventure journals that were published in the later nineteenth century and glamourised traditional masculinity in wild Empire settings, mainly for an audience of teenage boys and young men.[24] One design of this sort shows an Indian scene of a tiger attacking a man on horseback; another has an African scene with an angry big monkey biting at a man's arm; while yet another depicts a hunter in what seems to be a last ditch attempt at warding off a grizzly bear. Fox hunts with hounds, bison hunts and bull fights also feature in these colourful designs for male consumers [Figs. 4.29 to 4.32].

Figures and objects

The figurative and pictorial designs contained in the Museum's Turkey Red Collection are some of the most attractive to modern eyes, which is not surprising because many, as with the hunting scenes described above, were designed for themed handkerchiefs, where the simple square of fabric derived most of its value from the images that it bore. Figurative patterns include large numbers of commemorative designs, which were mostly aimed at European or British markets and celebrate significant events or prominent individuals. Portraits of famous people, such as the British-allied generals of the Crimean War or Queen Victoria, were copied from popular pictures in magazines and newspapers and reproduced as textile designs usually for short-run sales. In some cases these commemorative wares were sold as souvenirs of a specific event. One of the first known and widely described examples from the Scottish Turkey red industry was a handkerchief produced by William Stirling & Sons for the Great Exhibition of 1851. Though made in many thousands, none of these has survived, though a written account in the *Glasgow Herald* states that it included views of the Crystal Palace, images of Britannia,

Figure 4.29

Handkerchief designs could incorporate exotic themes, such as this one which shows a tiger attacking a horseman. John Orr Ewing & Co., mid-19th century.

Cotton; height 238 mm; width 305 mm

National Museums Scotland
A.1962.1266.25.1285

Figure 4.30

The somewhat violent imagery of these handkerchief designs suggests they were intended for male consumers. In this design an angry monkey can be seen biting the arm of a hunter. John Orr Ewing & Co., mid-19th century.

Cotton; height 252 mm; width 311 mm

National Museums Scotland
A.1962.1266.25.1186

Figure 4.31

As we can only see part of the design it can be difficult to know if it was meant to commemorate a particular event or not. This sample is from a book which dates from before 1866 and was probably intended for the North American market. John Orr Ewing & Co., mid-19th century.

Cotton; height 242 mm; width 290 mm

National Museums Scotland
A.1962.1266.25.1188

Figure 4.32

Nostalgic hunting scenes appear frequently on the surviving handkerchief designs. John Orr Ewing & Co., mid-19th century.

Cotton; height 242 mm; width 290 mm

National Museums Scotland
A.1962.1266.25.1106

classical imagery to represent art and industry, and various motifs to symbolize the four corners of the globe.²⁵ In 1887 a design was produced to commemorate Queen Victoria's Golden Jubilee. It also contained motifs that celebrated Britain and the Empire, including depictions of Britannia and the royal standards. [See Fig. 4.8]

British battles and victories during the Crimean and Boer Wars were celebrated in commemorative designs. The Crimean War (1853–1856) coincided with the first big expansion of the Turkey red industry, during a decade when commemorative wares for other types of occasion, such as the great exhibitions, had become popular. The Crimean War was the first to be followed by the modern media, giving rise to daily newspaper reports and even photographs, which impacted significantly on public awareness of battles, victories and losses, and fuelled a popular demand for reproduced scenes on all

Figure 4.33 (above)

There are a number of designs in the Turkey Red Collection which relate to the Crimean War, some depicting successful leaders [see Fig. 4.34], others giving details of particular battles. This sample shows a detail of the Battle of Inkerman in November 1854. It was probably produced by Robert Alexander and Co., just before John Orr Ewing came back into the industry, mid-19th century.

Cotton; height 250 mm; width 180 mm

National Museums Scotland A.1962.1266.1.84 A

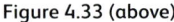

Figure 4.34 (above, right)

There were two men with the rank and name of Admiral Dundas in the Crimean War – James Whitley Deans Dundas and Richard Saunders Dundas – thus it is not clear which individual this image represents. This design was an ephemeral one and would have been produced either during or shortly after the Crimean War. Unidentified Vale of Leven firm, mid-19th century.

Cotton; height 238 mm; width 234 mm

National Museums Scotland A.1962.1266.6.20.535

manner of commercially produced goods, including textiles. One handkerchief design for John Orr Ewing & Co., or R. Alexander & Co., shows the November 1854 Battle of Inkerman, which was a victory for British and French forces over the Russian enemy [Fig. 4.33]. The design, which may have been copied from a newspaper plan of the battlefield, shows a series of vignettes of key events during the course of the Inkerman engagement, with a numbered interpretive key at the bottom with titles such as '10: French reinforcements going into action'; '11: Russian infantry'; or '14: 2 gun battery'. Another Crimean War handkerchief depicts the military hero Admiral Dundas – one of two possible candidates with the same name, both leaders of naval operations in the Black Sea and both subsequently rewarded with the Order of the Bath, which appears in the portrait along with ships and boats, with circlets of daisy-like flowers and foliage [Fig. 4.34]. Depictions of Boer War battles, which saw massive mobilisation of British troops to fight a war of Empire in far-away South Africa, were particularly poignant for workers at the Turkey red factories in the Vale of Leven because many men who worked there volunteered for military service, which their employer supported. In October 1899, for instance, the United Turkey Red Co. Ltd Board of Directors agreed to pay the sum of 10s weekly to the wives or families of Army Reserve Men in the employment of the company who had been called out on foreign service. They also agreed to pay the reservists the same bonus at the end of the year that they might have been paid had they remained at home. Notices declaring these resolutions were posted on the gates of the various works in the company, as an act of patriotic support for the war effort and for the encouragement of other potential enlistees.[26]

Other sorts of events represented in commemorative designs included the anniversaries of famous tragedies. One sample in the Museum's Turkey Red Collection, for instance, in production by John Orr Ewing & Co. up to the 1860s, shows the stern of a sinking ship with the name 'Kent' on the side and passengers scrambling into a lifeboat [Fig. 4.35]. This is a reference to the famous loss of the East Indiaman *Kent*, which went down after a fire in the Bay of Biscay en route to Calcutta in March 1825, with a passenger list that was dominated by soldiers and their families. The *Kent* tragedy saw great heroism amongst the crew, but also loss of life, including women and children. Numerous works of art commemorate the event, which was also the subject of a popular Edinburgh-published personal account of the same year by General Sir Duncan McGregor titled *A Narrative of the Loss of the Kent East Indiaman … In a Letter to a Friend, by a Passenger*, which was reissued in 1880 by McGregor's son, who had been an infant on the ship.[27] Engraved images and written accounts

Figure 4.35

The East Indiaman *Kent* sank after a fire in 1825. It was widely reported in the British press and became the subject of numerous works of art and accounts. This design was produced many decades later, probably to mark an anniversary. John Orr Ewing & Co., mid-19th century.

Cotton; height 238 mm; width 234 mm

National Museums Scotland
A.1962.1266.25.1189

Figure 4.36

These unusual designs commemorate the introduction of the Queen Victoria Rupee to India in 1862. Some of these designs were placed under copyright in 1863. John Orr Ewing & Co., 1862.

Cotton; height 150 mm; width: 137 mm (each sample approx.)

National Museums Scotland A.1962.1266.29.1304

appeared at intervals throughout the century.[28] The '*Kent* tragedy' formed the subject of an article in the *Boy's Own Paper* in 1894 and was even commemorated in a popular poem of 1900 from the pen of William McGonagall, who performed music hall recitals throughout Scotland on the same theme.

Unsurprisingly, representations of Queen Victoria feature regularly in the Museum's Turkey Red Collection, particularly on flags designed for the Jubilee years of 1887 and 1897, many customised for export to the different countries of the Empire. One of the early and more unusual patterns is a small-print design of circles containing the monarch's profile bust, which was issued in 1862 to celebrate the first introduction of the Queen Victoria Rupee to India [Fig. 4.36]. There are a number of variations on this design, which John Orr Ewing & Co. placed under copyright in 1863. Other rulers depicted in commemorative prints include King George I of Greece, who was of Danish-German birth, on the occasion of his accession in 1863, which was supported by the British state; and Isma'il Pasha, Khedive of Egypt and Sudan – which was another area of the eastern Mediterranean that was of strategic interest for Britain, this time focused on the Suez Canal – who made a state visit to London in 1867 [Fig. 4.37].

Most of the human figures that appear in Turkey red patterns were male, reflecting the common use of these types of prints in handkerchiefs and bandannas, which were mostly consumed by men. The 'animal attack' handkerchiefs mentioned above all involve attacks on men and frequently also include weapon such as rifles or spears in the decorative borders. In a handkerchief pattern in red, black and white registered for copyright by Archibald Orr Ewing & Co. in

Figure 4.37

Before a design could be put on the fabric it had to be sketched out on paper. This sketch celebrates the relationship between Britain and Egypt during the years leading to the opening of the Suez Canal in 1869. It depicts the Khedive of Egypt during a European tour. Possibly created by William Stirling & Sons, mid-19th century.

Paper; height 288 mm; width 200 mm

National Museums Scotland A.1962.1266.28.2.3757

Figure 4.38

With its clear Masonic symbolism this is one of the most unusual designs of the collection. It is a 'strike-off' showing how the form of a pattern looks on paper before it is tried on fabric. It is also from one of the earliest pattern books in the Turkey Red Collection, dating from 1843. William Stirling & Sons, 1843 to late 19th century.

Paper; height 265 mm; width 209 mm

National Museums Scotland
A.1962.1266.31.5.448

Figure 4.39

Like the black and white Masonic design, this one appears to be relatively early and probably dates from the mid-19th century. John Orr Ewing & Co., mid-19th century.

Cotton; height 505 mm; width 314 mm

National Museums Scotland
A.1962.1266.25.1122

1879, a collection of arrows, a spear and what appears to be an axe or tomahawk are printed in each corner of the design. An example of the same handkerchief with different colouring is in the collection of the Philadelphia Museum of Art and is described as being of French manufacture, intended for export to the French Congo.[29] The assumption is that Archibald Orr Ewing & Co. either purchased the design from France or, just as likely, simply copied it for reproduction as a

Turkey red print. Two designs in the Museum's Turkey Red Collection that reflect a different aspect of Victorian masculine culture are those containing Masonic symbols. The first is an early black and white design on paper, probably produced by William Stirling & Sons and featuring a skeleton, beehive, crossed keys and various other ritual symbols, such as the 'all-seeing' eye and clasped hands [Fig. 4.38]. The second is a handkerchief design from the 1870s, which includes a compass, globe, coffin and pillar [Fig. 4.39]. The purpose of these designs is unclear. They may have been used in Freemason's ceremonies, but just as likely were for retail sale to practising masons at home or abroad, particularly in North America.[30]

While male figures dominated in certain export markets, figurative designs for India included many women, be they mythical, 'real' or religious. The traditional dancing girl (or *nautch* motif) appears in numerous forms, the most common being the imitation tie-dye made up of small, mosaic-like squares [Fig. 4.40]. The use of dancing figures was a feature of Indian art since antiquity and considered 'one of the highest forms in the representation of divine power'.[31] Shiva, a male deity and the Hindu god of destruction, is also shown dancing and appears in some prints. Other Hindu religious figures reproduced on Scottish Turkey red designs include the goddess Lakshmi, holding a lotus in one hand and a small gold pot in another, [see Fig. 4.2] on a John Orr Ewing & Co. shawl, and Krishna, depicted as a young boy playing the flute, in a design that was copyrighted by William Stirling & Sons in 1884.[32] Children appear in various patterns, including those with Chinese influence. A handkerchief design on paper made for John Orr Ewing & Co. in 1882 includes a centrepiece of three oriental children at play, one riding a hobbyhorse, surrounded by floral motifs and trailing vines [see Fig. 4.41]. Acrobats and jugglers form the filling of the pattern for a similar 'oriental' handkerchief, with the border made up of parrots and flowers.[33] Other oriental figures include samurai fighters and Japanese lady with a fan on a curious print, probably for home sale, that is designed to look like patchwork.[34]

Aside from depictions of humans and

Figure 4.40

Although cylinder printing was generally used to produce intricate designs, there are still examples of complex block printed patterns within the Turkey Red Collection. This imitation tie-dye design shows the dancing girl in the filling, with a border of peacocks, flowers and geometric patterns. A different block would have been used for each colour of the pattern. John Orr Ewing & Co., late 19th century.

Cotton; height 470 mm; width 302 mm

National Museums Scotland A.1962.1266.16.6.11

Figure 4.41

The textile designs sometimes come with labels attached during the design or manufacturing process. This one is painted onto paper and the labels at the bottom indicate that the design was to be produced for a specific order in May 1882. It then gives the details of the sizes of the plates and cylinders used to produce the pattern. John Orr Ewing & Co., 1882.

Paper; height 618 mm; width 620 mm

National Museums Scotland
A.1962.1266.27.1.5223

Figure 4.42

This is one of the larger examples from the Turkey Red Collection and could have been intended as a napkin or small table cloth. It comes from a furnishing fabric pattern book which is thought to have been used by Archibald Orr Ewing & Co. in the 1880s.

Cotton; height 464 mm; width 518 mm

National Museums Scotland
A.1962.1266.20.4.180

deities, the Turkey red prints include a range of inanimate images. Some are of day-to-day (or at least recognisable) things such as a wine carafe and glasses, in a design probably intended to be used as a tablecloth [Fig. 4.42], or the lead plate printed design of an anchor and chain. In other instances a recognizable shape, such as a fan or parasol, is reproduced in a regular pattern arrangement. A design produced at some point between the 1860s and the 1880s, which looks as though

it was probably used for Indian sari end pieces or for shawls, has a multi-coloured steam train as the centre piece, surrounded by multi-coloured flowers, peacocks and paisley shapes. This pattern may have served a commemorative function, marking perhaps the opening of a major railway line in India. Whatever its purpose, it represented a significant departure from the normal conservative taste favoured in India and doubtless drew comments when worn [Fig. 4.43].

Abstract and geometric

As with the floral, figurative and animal designs, abstract and geometric patterns could cater to all the different domestic and foreign markets that were served by the Scottish Turkey red industry [Fig 4.44]. They sometimes consist of imitation tie-dye patterns in geometric formations, checks and spots, straight lines and undulating lines, often with another style of decorative motif incorporated, such as flowers

Figure 4.43 (above, left)

As a global industry producing goods with many complex cultural influences, it is not surprising that hybrid styles and motifs were thrown together for novelty effect. In this design, peacocks and paisley motifs are used as the border for a multi-coloured steam train. This pattern was taken out of production in 1868. Unidentified Vale of Leven firm, mid-19th century.

Cotton; height 370 mm; width 295 mm

National Museums Scotland A.1962.1266.31.9.627

Figure 4.44 (right)

Geometric patterns were often used for sari pieces. Concentric squares, as seen in the sari here, appear a number of times in the Turkey Red Collection. This photograph shows a *nautch* or dancing girl. Charles Shepherd, c.1862.

© The British Library Board, India Office Select Materials, photo 28/2 (24)

printed over a ground of spots or checks. Geometric prints were particularly popular in the Indian market among Muslim consumers, who had a cultural antipathy to figurative representations on dress. This focus can be seen very clearly in the so-called 'mobile museum' of James Forbes Watson, which comprised Indian textile samples in volumes, which were sent to the various manufacturing centres of Great Britain to inform designers and entrepreneurs of popular Indian patterns and the specific regional and religious markets. With a sophisticated hand-weaving culture, it is not surprising that the most common group of Indian textiles presented by Forbes Watson comprised woven checks and stripes, which were, of course, also popular in the British market.[35]

A Turkey red printed geometric pattern, which was based on Indian tie-dye and appears often in the Museum's collection, is the repeated zigzag on a red ground. This is known as *leheriya* in India and is commonly used in men's turbans in Rajasthan.[36] A typical colour combination is yellow zigzags on a red ground, but other colour variations include a version that utilised the 'rainbow' printing technique, which had been developed in the early nineteenth century and allowed colours to blend together [Fig. 4.45]. The Scottish Turkey red manufacturers sometimes used a printing technique to give the impression of a more expensive woven fabric, with lines of diamond shapes, small checks and chevrons printed across the width of the cloth. One example has the overall effect of Scottish tartan, which would have been familiar in India from the large numbers of Scottish regiments that were stationed there, and it is not surprising that tartan textiles found a ready market in this part of the Empire, though not, of course, made in wool, which was too hot for India [Figs. 4.46 and 4.47].

Figure 4.45

The Turkey red manufacturers were not afraid to combine traditional styles and patterns with modern printing techniques. Here the zigzag effect is reminiscent of the leheriya tie-dye technique, but the 'rainbowing' effect came from a modern printing technique that was popular in the mid-19th century. John Orr Ewing & Co., post-1870.

Cotton; height 142 mm; width 296 mm

National Museums Scotland
A.1962.1266.16.2.668

Figure 4.46 (above)

Textile printing was often used to imitate more complex decorative techniques, such as weaving or embroidery. In this case the fabric is printed to make it look like it has been woven from different coloured threads. A similar pattern can be seen in Fig. 4.48. William Stirling & Sons, United Turkey Red Co. Ltd., 1889–98.

Cotton; height 280 mm; width 187 mm

National Museums Scotland A.1962.1266.9.16.690

Figure 4.47 (above, right)

The scarf worn by this man is probably woven, but the pattern at the end of the cloth is similar to that of 4.47 and other samples in the Turkey Red Collection. Photograph of a schoff or native banker from John Forbes Watson's *The People of India*, volume 6 (1872), image 330.

Courtesy of Edinburgh University Library, ref: S.B.F.572 (54) Wat

Figure 4.48 (below)

This is a complex design with a checked filling and floral border. The shades of the colours and the overall style indicate that it is an early example of a handkerchief pattern. William Stirling & Sons, *c.*1845–1855.

Cotton; height 315 mm; width 235 mm

National Museums Scotland A.1962.1266.1.90 B

Figure 4.49

Although not as popular as floral shapes, abstract and geometric patterns lent themselves well to furnishing fabrics. This pattern is from a furniture pattern book. We know that the book was used after 1876 thanks to a stationer's label in the front cover. Unidentified Vale of Leven firm, post 1876.

Cotton; height 505 mm; width 602 mm

National Museums Scotland A.1962.1266.21.1.4194

Abstract and geometric designs were produced for many domestic and western markets – a number of handkerchiefs, for instance, consist of floral borders with checked fillings, which also served well for patterns for protective garments like aprons or children's clothes [Fig. 4.48]. The Turkey red manufacturers mainly followed established trends, and included the reproduction of variations of such innovative designs as 'Lane's Net', a geometric quasi-three dimensional pattern of the 1840s, which enjoy a longstanding popularity.[37] 'Lane's net' was described by one contemporary as a 'particular style of design known by the name of "eccentrics"' and was thought to be a British innovation. The design was easily pirated without prosecution:

> Copyright protects the pattern and not the style; so that a really good and new design opens up a mine of ideas for the whole trade, which they may work simultaneously, provided they do not infringe the original design.[38]

This, of course, favoured the Turkey red companies who, as we have seen, were great copiers and 'pirates' [Fig. 4.49].

Notes

1. Sonia Ashmore, 'Owen Jones and the V&A Collections', *V&A Online Journal*, 1 (2008).
2. *Edinburgh Review*, April 1869, pp. 386–87, 'Reports of the Paris Universal Exhibition'.
3. *Journal of Design and Manufactures*, vol. v, 1851, p.7 5, Archibald Orr Ewing & Co. print; vol vi, 1852, p. 8, William Stirling & Sons Swiss chintz velvet print.
4. Rosemary Crill, *Chintz: Indian Textiles for the West* (London, 2008), p. 21.
5. Sonia Ashmore, *Muslin* (London, 2012), p. 20; Madeleine Ginsburg, *The Illustrated History of Textiles* (London, 1991), p. 58.
6. See Chapter 3.
7. See, for example, Robert Tyas, *The Sentiment of Flowers: Or, Language of Flora* (London, 1836), and numerous subsequent editions.
8. Paul Hulton and Lawrence Smith, *Flowers in Art from East and West* (London, 1979), p. ix.
9. Linda Lynton, *The Sari: Styles, Patterns, History, Techniques* (London, 2002), p. 161.
10. Ibid, p. 169.
11. Dr Philip Sykas of Manchester Metropolitan University has matched a design from National Museums Scotland's Turkey Red Collection with a sarong shown in a 19th-century photograph of a young Tahitian girl.
12. Valerie Reilly, *The Paisley Pattern. The Official Illustrated History* (Glasgow, 1987).
13. John Irwin, *The Kashmir Shawl* (London, 1973), p. 19.
14. Francina Irwin, 'Scottish eighteenth-century chintz and its design', *Burlington Magazine*, 107: 750 (1965), pp. 452–58.
15. See Chapter 3.
16. See Lynton, *The Sari*, p. 176.
17. Ginsburg, *Illustrated History of Textiles*, p. 78.
18. S. Cheang, 'Dragons in the drawing room: Chinese embroideries in British homes, 1860–1949', *Textile History*, 24: 2 (2008), p. 244.
19. E. Kramer, 'Master or market? The Anglo-Japanese textile designs of Christopher Dresser', *Journal of Design History*, 19: 3 (2006), pp. 197–214.
20. C. A. S. Williams, *Chinese Symbolism and Art Motifs: A Comprehensive Handbook on Symbolism in Chinese Art Through the Ages* (Vermont, 2006), pp. 118–19.
21. C. A. S. Williams, *Outline of Chinese Symbolism and Art Motifs* (New York, 1976), pp. 51–52, p. 323.
22. William Floor, *The Persian Textile Industry in Historical Perspective, 1500–1925* (Paris, 1999), pp. 245–46.
23. Rudolf Wittkower, 'Eagle and serpent: a study in the migration of symbols', *Journal of the Warburg Institute*, 2: 4 (1939), pp. 293–325.
24. See, Kelly Boyd, *Manliness and the Boys' Story Paper in Britain. A Cultural History* (London, 2003).
25. *Glasgow Herald*, 21 February 1851.
26. MCRO: UTR Minute Book no. 2, 18 October 1899.
27. *Glasgow Herald*, 4 November 1880.
28. As in Thomas Carter, *Perils at Sea* (London, 1859).
29. Philadelphia Museum of Art. Accession number 2004–111–8.
30. Embroidered and quilted masonic textiles were popular in North America and were the subject of a 2012 exhibition at the Scottish Rites and Masonic Museum and Library in Lexington, USA.
31. Heinz Mode, *The Woman in Indian Art* (Leipzig, 1970), p. 8, p. 31.
32. This design is held in the Board of Trade Design Registers, the National Archives at Kew, but does not survive in Museum's pattern book collection.
33. National Museums Scotland: Turkey Red Collection. Accession no. A.1962.1266.9.5.6743.
34. National Museums Scotland: Turkey Red Collection. Accession no. A.1962.1266.9.5.6677.
35. F. Driver and S. Ashmore, 'The mobile museum. Collecting and circulating Indian textiles in Victorian Britain', *Victorian Studies* 52: 3 (2010).
36. Nasreen Askari and Liz Arthur, *Uncut Cloth: Saris, Shawls and Sashes* (London, 1999), p. 65.
37. Kriegel, *Grand Designs*, p. 78.
38. *The Art Union*, April 15, 1841. 'Copyright in design.'

CHAPTER FIVE

International markets

THE BRITISH cotton industry, which was the lead manufacturing sector in the first industrial revolution, relied on overseas sources of raw cotton, mainly from North America but also India and the Middle East, and the success of the industry was based mostly on exports. The industry slowly died in the twentieth century because other countries developed their own modern factories and because international markets were flooded by cheaper products from countries like India and Japan.

In the early years of the British industry the main export markets were in Europe and North America, but Europe invested in the development of its own industry and America, with control of raw cotton production, soon became a technical innovator and mass producer. The shift in export emphasis inevitably moved to the east and to the countries of the British Empire and India in particular. Most of Britain's cotton exports were of low quality 'grey' fabrics for dyeing and printing elsewhere, or, increasingly, cotton yarn for weaving abroad. The British printed cotton industry was not generally competitive in international sales of fine dyed and printed goods, the exception being that of Turkey red textiles, where a few firms with great sophistication in their dyeing and printing techniques were able to produce a colour-fast deep red fabric that found commercial favour abroad.[1]

Awareness of the varying characters of the international markets, for designs and patterns, and for different weights and qualities of cloth, was a mainstay of the Turkey red industry, and casual observers were often struck by the varieties seen in factory production. An 1844 *Penny Magazine* article about Henry Monteith & Co.'s famous Barrowfield printworks in Glasgow observed that the Chinese market required 'patterns in which natural objects such as birds and flowers are depicted', but also noted that blue was the favoured colour for cotton goods for this trade. The South American countries, who were major consumers, desired a 'gorgeous mix of colours … large masses of bright red, blue and yellow – without any particular

Opposite page:

A sarong that is a sample of flat press printed cotton cloth (see Fig. 5.12).

National Museums Scotland

reference to the pattern'. Closer to home, German customers wanted 'pictorial subjects … copied from celebrated works of art by Overbeck [and] Cornelius', as well as representations of 'cathedrals, abbeys, castles and public buildings'. Patterns for domestic sale, however, were

> … generally unmeaning, representing objects which never have existed and never will; curves, zigzags, stripes, spots, all imaginable shapes are combined together into patterns, which are pleasing, perhaps, to the eye, but have no definite meaning.[2]

The report ended with the astute observation that 'a sixpenny handkerchief may, if we choose to study it rightly, be made the means of giving us a little insight into national character and taste'. The article failed to mention the trade with North America, which had been important up to the 1820s, and the prominence of the Indian and South East Asian market was still some years in the future.

North America

Printed cotton goods were exported to North America for decades before the Turkey red process was first introduced to Scotland in the later eighteenth century. 'Scotch handkerchiefs' in checks and spots with borders, along with coloured threads, were a staple export to Virginia and North Carolina, where there were large migrant Scottish populations, and were advertised in commercial journals such as the *Pennsylvania Gazette*. The North American trade benefited from familial and business links that were established through colonial tobacco production, with Scottish-owned stores selling a range of basic manufactured goods to plantation owners, such as clothing and household textiles, in return for their tobacco crops, which were then sent for processing in Scotland. Though this privileged connection ended in the revolution of 1776, a tradition of Scottish trading links survived for decades. This can be seen in advertisements for the company Gordon, Trokes, Leitch & Co. of New York, which had Liverpool and Glasgow-based partners, and sold various textiles in September 1810, recently arrived on the ship *George*, including, 'One trunk of Turkey red bandanna handkerchiefs of different sizes'.[3]

Bandannas, a mainstay of the Scottish Turkey red industry, were hemmed pieces of square red cloth, larger than a handkerchief and smaller than a shawl, and usually about 23-inch or 25-inch squared. Their most iconic association was with the North American cowboy, but they were worn by working men and women of all occupations in a variety of ways.⁴ They had simple white patterns of dots or diamonds with contrasting borders. Originating in India, they were first produced using tie-dye techniques, which were then copied using modern machine methods whereby the whole cloth was first dyed red and then a pattern of white was created through the 'discharge' of dye with a substance known as 'chloride of lime' [Fig. 5.1]. Henry Monteith & Co. of Glasgow, the greatest of the bandanna manufacturers, was celebrated for its ability to produce 224 handkerchiefs or bandannas in ten minutes, which were then exported across the world.⁵

Figure 5.1

A typical bandanna pattern with white dots in the filling and a striped border. Other examples had small diamond or club shapes in the filling. John Orr Ewing & Co., mid-19th century.

Cotton; height 190 mm; width 288 mm

National Museums Scotland A.1962.1266.25.849

Advertisements for bandannas appear regularly in American journals during the late eighteenth and early nineteenth century, along with notices for Turkey red handkerchiefs and shawls. In 1797 William Leckie of New York told his customers that he had received printed Turkey red handkerchiefs, among other things, from his partners in Glasgow, who he said were the manufacturers of these goods and as such he flattered 'himself that he can make them as low [in price] as any in the city'.⁶ Similar items were shipped to the West Indies, for use as headscarves and neckerchiefs by slaves on the sugar plantations, many owned by Scots. Turkey red printed shawls from Glasgow and from Europe, sometimes embellished with fringes, were also advertised in the American press, often in imitation of more expensive handwoven Paisley shawls.

References to Turkey red fabric, both plain and printed, can be found in all manner of nineteenth-century American publications, giving a sense of how it was used and how it was valued. In an edition of *Godey's Lady's Book and Magazine* from 1866, an article described the dress of women in the southern states during the American Civil War, which had ended just a year earlier. The writer recalled that before the war, women had brightened their everyday dress with pieces of Turkey red, but the war had meant that they had become increasingly reliant on the 'poor, dingy colours' of their home-made dyes.⁷ In August 1895, an article which described the studio of artist Daniel C. Beard noted that one of the most interesting objects in the room was a Confederate flag, captured by Beard's brother during the Civil War and sent home as a souvenir. The flag was made of two stripes of Turkey red fabric and one stripe of fine white linen.⁸ Before the outbreak of the war in 1861, much of the cotton used by the Vale of Leven firms had originated in the southern states of America. The war effectively halted this trade, which meant the Vale firms had to rely increasingly on their Indian suppliers. This did not stop one firm from cashing in on the American situation. In 1864, John Orr Ewing & Co. sent a design to the Board of Trade in London that they wished to be placed under copyright protection. This design was essentially the Confederate flag of a diagonal blue and white cross on a red ground. The only difference was that the stars within the cross were yellow rather than white.[9] Whether or not the design was actually intended for the American market or for purchase by Confederate supporters in Britain is not known. Other flags that were produced for North America included the 'stars and stripes' in its various forms and also the 'informal' Canadian flag – a Union Jack and Provinces Shield on a red ensign – which appears prominently in one of the Museum's patterns books and was exported in large numbers for patriotic display during the Queen Victoria Diamond Jubilee celebrations of 1897, along with flags depicting the Queen and the royal coat of arms [Figs 5.2 and 5.3].

Figure 5.2

This example has two pieces of cloth glued on top of one another to show two different parts of a design produced for the Canadian market to celebrate Queen Victoria's Diamond Jubilee in 1897. The symbols on the coat of arms include the St George Cross, golden maple leaves, a lion, thistle, galley and fish, and they relate to the armorial bearings of Quebec, New Brunswick and Ontario, granted by Queen Victoria in the 1860s. John Orr Ewing & Co., 1897.

Cotton; height 265 mm; width 270 mm

National Museums Scotland A.1962.1266.10.3.4093

Figure 5.3

Photographs of Turkey red textiles in the 19th century are rare. This one is particularly interesting as it shows the full flag design of Fig 5.2, to the right of the door, along with other patriotic flags which were used to decorate a house in Canada during Queen Victoria's Diamond Jubilee in 1897. Photo showing Koshaqua Lodge, 5th Street, Sturgeon Point, Ontario, Canada.

With kind permission of the Sturgeon Point History Project, Brown Family Collection

Turkey red dyed and printed cottons were commonly used for children's clothing, as is often shown in American folk art portraits from the early to mid-nineteenth century.[10] Other advertised uses included the lining for a lady's jacket to be worn when mountain climbing[11] and cushion covers for outdoor furniture.[12] The fabric was hard-wearing and did not show dirt, a virtue highlighted by a Maine country housewife in a newspaper letter of 1884 titled 'Washing made easy'.

> Let me say first, that I economize the washing as much as possible by the use of a turkey red table cloth for common, and neither I, nor my little girl, indulge in white skirts, or light dresses, except upon special occasions.[13]

Turkey red printed cottons found their way into other types of home furnishings. Surviving examples of nineteenth-century quilts in private and museum collections show that the small print patterns with simplified, repeated flowers and paisley shapes were a popular choice for the block style and sampler quilts of the mid-nineteenth-century American household.[14] Plain Turkey red was also used in quilts, providing a strong contrast with lighter coloured fabrics. These quilts, the product of many hours of work, often undertaken communally as gifts to celebrate a marriage, and including complex designs and motifs, are probably the largest group of surviving artefacts which demonstrate how Turkey red dyed and printed fabrics were used in the nineteenth century [Figs 5.4 and 5.5]. But without dye analysis it is impossible to determine if the surviving examples of Turkey red fabrics contained in quilts were made in Scotland or in North America. Certainly, from early in the nineteenth century there were attempts to reproduce the Turkey red dyeing process locally, sometimes even in domestic contexts. An example was reported in the July 1811 edition of *The Archives of Useful Knowledge, A Work Devoted to Commerce, Manufacturers, Rural and Domestic Economy*:

> Mrs Washington [of Winchester, Virginia] made attempt last summer to dye cotton to the colour generally known by the name of Turkey Red. She followed a receipt contained in the *Domestic Encyclopaedia*, and succeeded beyond her expectations in imparting to the cotton yarn a beautiful, brilliant red colour, possessing a permanence that was at first little expected. She had the yarn woven into a piece of fancy cloth, for her own wear, which has been very often washed, and still retains its brilliancy of colour, without any sensible diminution …. Happy the country gentleman, whose wife is occupied in such pursuits!

Figure 5.4

Turkey red dyed and printed cottons were often used in quilts in the 19th century. There are numerous examples from the east coast of America, including this signature or friendship quilt which was made by a member of the Clayton family in the Delaware Valley in the early 1840s. There are 42 signatures on the quilt.

Courtesy, Winterthur Museum, pieced friendship quilt. Gift of Thomas Reed Clayton and family, 2003.53

Figure 5.5

The small print patterns of the Turkey red industry lent themselves well to decorative furnishing fabrics and had the added advantage of being resistant to fading from sunlight and washing. There are 29 different small print patterns used in this quilt, along with 27 signatures.

Courtesy, Winterthur Museum, quilt top. Gift of William and Ellen Styer, 2010.21.1

While British Turkey red was still being advertised in the American press, by mid-century American-produced printed cottons were on the increase, along with advice on the local production of the raw materials needed for the dyeing industry.[15] The long-running and popular journal *Scientific American*, founded in 1845, carried many reports on inventions and patents in Europe, including those relating to the textile industry, and the edition for 17 September 1881 gave a lengthy recipe for dyeing Turkey red using the natural madder-based process. By 1887 the *Textile Manufacturers' Directory of the United States and Canada* was listing five major firms as Turkey red manufacturers and it seems likely that there were other smaller concerns that also experimented with the process. One of the biggest companies, famous in its day, was the Clyde Print Works and Bleachery of Rhode Island.[16] First founded in the eighteenth century, this business, as the name suggests, had long established connections with Scotland, and in 1867 they 'headhunted' a new works manager from Glasgow. Robert Reoch, born near Glasgow in 1840, was the son and grandson of calico printers, who began his career with an apprenticeship in the Fereneze Print Works at Barrhead in Renfrewshire, progressing to the post of assistant manager in their colouring department. He took chemistry lessons at Glasgow University before moving to Muir, Brown & Co., a firm of Turkey red dyers, to run their print works. Having been tempted to emigrate to the United States, Reoch pioneered the introduction of the Turkey red process to the Clyde Print Works in Rhode Island, with a line of celebrated flags, bandannas and commemorative handkerchiefs, as well as mass-produced plain red and well-designed prints, that transformed the fortunes of the company. These can still be seen in museum collections today. At his death in 1918, Reoch was widely lauded as one of the great pioneers and innovators in the modern American textile industry.[17]

By the end of the nineteenth century, the United States produced its own printed cottons and Scottish firms could no longer compete on price in this market. There is no recorded evidence of United States exports in the surviving business records of the Vale of Leven firms, but links with Canada were maintained, although doubtless this colonial market was also supplied from elsewhere in America. A so-called 'home sales book' for William Stirling & Sons, which covers the six months from January to June 1895, includes three Canadian companies in the list of merchants and contacts that the firm supplied. These were Hodgshon Sumner & Co. of Montreal, Stobart Sons & Co. of Manitoba, and Thomas Watkins of Hamilton, all major wholesalers.[18]

But if the North American export market had all but died by the later decades of the century, the influence of American culture was still evident in some of the distinctive Turkey red designs that were produced for sale in Britain. The popularity of the 'wild west', known through illustrated books and magazines, and through touring cowboys and Indians shows – the most famous being the great travelling circus of Colonel 'Buffalo Bill' Cody, which first visited Glasgow in 1892 – was reflected in the reproduction of print designs that included cowboys on horseback, and hunting scenes with buffaloes and bears [Fig. 5.6]. Other American influenced designs, which were possibly also exported, include a repeated white turkey motif on a two red ground, which may have been used for tablecloths for

Figure 5.6

A handkerchief design depicting a horseman shooting a bison or a buffalo. John Orr Ewing & Co., mid-19th century.

Cotton; height 250 mm; width 310 mm

National Museums Scotland
A.1962.1266.25.1187

Thanksgiving celebrations [see Fig. 4.26]. There also exists, perhaps influenced by or for the Mexican market, a print that shows the design of an eagle and a snake, the national symbols of Mexico that still feature on the flag today [see Fig. 4.22].

India

The Turkey red cotton industry was predominantly an export industry. Its biggest market was India, a vast sub-continent, the 'jewel in the crown' of the British Empire, a destination for many Scottish soldiers and merchants, and long a source of fashionable luxuries imported through the East India Company. Indian demand, which at its height in the 1880s absorbed 60 per cent of British cotton exports, was mainly for plain textiles, which were dyed and printed by local craftsmen in traditional and subtle designs and colours to meet Indian tastes. The only area of British high-value dyed and printed cotton manufacture that competed effectively in India was that produced by the technically complex Turkey red industry.[19] Red was a cultural signifier of celebration and good luck throughout Asia, but was difficult to make using small-scale craft techniques. It was only with the wide availability of the synthetic dye alizarin at the end of the century, that India's reliance on imported red textiles and yarn began to change. India was not only the focus for exports of printed cottons, it also received vast quantities of plain Turkey red fabric of different types and qualities; much of it was for further processing, using acids to bleach out the colour for local over-printing with wood blocks. India imported large quantities of Turkey red dyed cotton yarn for local weaving, a trade that grew as the century progressed and inevitably

Figure 5.7

Bombay cotton merchant and bales of Indian-grown raw cotton wool awaiting export, photographed in the second half of the 19th century by Francis Frith. Whole-plate albumen print from wet collodion glass negative.

© Victoria and Albert Museum, London

undermined British industry. Moreover, India as a cotton producer was the source of raw cotton for manufacture in Britain, particularly in the 1860s when American supplies were halted by the Civil War [Fig. 5.7].

Indian-inspired designs are seen throughout the Museum's pattern books and dominated the output of all of the companies involved in the Turkey red industry. These are usually reproduced in yellow, orange and green on red. Patterns include sari borders, borders for turbans, choli blouse patterns and styles specified as suitable for collars and shawls. Patterns designed for different ethnic and religious groups are also commonly indicated. Other iconic Scottish textiles, in particular the Paisley shawl industry, also made extensive use of Indian design motifs, which first came to Britain in the eighteenth century as fashionable and expensive imported Indian cotton chintzes or Kashmir woollen and silk shawls.

Bombay was the focus for exports from the Scottish Turkey red industry to India in the 1850s and 1860s, as the existence in the Museum's collection of the Bombay Pattern Book attests [see Fig. 1.4]. The Bombay Pattern Book, one of the few to include samples with accompanying text descriptions and dates, was compiled by the firm of William Stirling & Sons between 1853 and 1868, probably in their Glasgow offices; it mostly comprises letters from agents in Bombay making orders, supplying samples for copying and providing market information on sales in the bazaars. A typical entry, with samples, was sent by one of their main agents, the Swiss-founded Huschke & Co., and dated 28 February 1858. It stated, 'The brightness of the colour and the styles of the print are very much admired in our market'. One sample is 'submitted especially to show [you the] finish of the cloth these being very much liked by our dealers'.[20]

The Bombay Pattern Book was created at a time when John Matheson was the active partner in William Stirling & Sons.[21] Matheson is remarkable for having made two lengthy visits to India during the course of his career, for pleasure but also to investigate in person the main destination for his company's exports. The first trip in 1861, via the arduous overland route, was later published as a travel account.[22] His second trip in the early 1870s was by sea via the Suez Canal. Matheson, who was accompanied by his wife on the first trip, travelled to India with a Glasgow business friend, William Mackinnon, a shipping entrepreneur. Mackinnon's interests in India at this time were to petition government officials to be allowed to create a new shipping line from Bombay to Calcutta, an initiative that was designed to further his own commercial ambitions as well as aiding the export interests of his friends.[23]

Matheson's *England to Delhi: A Narrative of Indian Travel*, published in 1870, provides a vivid and entertaining account of the sights and people of India in the early 1860s, just a few years after the East India Company had ceased operations. Matheson, as with most visitors to India, was entranced by what he saw; he was a great admirer of Indian craft textiles, providing many descriptions of manufacturers and the clothing worn by different local groups [Fig. 5.8]. In Agra, for instance, he observed:

Figure 5.8

Photograph of dyers in western India. The vats are sunk into the ground but unlike the copper vats seen by Matheson, these dyers are using vats made of clay. This image was shown at the Vienna Exhibition of 1873. Photograph by Shivashanker Narayan, 1873, from the Archaeological Survey of India Collection.

© The British Library Board

> Among the industries of the place, that of dyeing cotton cloth in purple and yellow colours appeared to be in extensive operation. The process was effected in the open shop by means of copper vessels sunk in the floor, the warehouse, or place for storing goods and transacting business, being, as in the similar shops of Delhi, the spaces between. It is a well-known fact that the goods thus prepared and sold in premises of such small compass are not less brilliant in hue than those which are dipped by steam revolving apparatus in the great vats of British manufactories, and find buyers in the trade palaces of London, Manchester, or Glasgow. It NEED scarcely be told that the tradespeople of India, however small the wages they earn, are clever craftsmen.[24]

But Matheson was also a businessman looking to his own commercial interest, and he welcomed what he saw as a growing dominance in India of imported, factory-made textiles such as those produced in his own factory in the Vale of Leven.

> Dyers and calico printers of India impart dyed colours and designs, in accordance with the native taste, to goods both of native and foreign make — to the tanta cloth and to Manchester shirtings. They are also accustomed to print their own patterns on British dyed fabrics, making use of an acid to extract the colour in styles where that process is necessary to produce the required effect. Thus, while revolving in wide, lofty chambers, the swift cylinder machines of Manchester and Glasgow are turning off each one 600 yards of cloth (more or less) per hour, the manufacturing industry of India jogs slowly along in little holes and corners, after its own primitive plan; both classes of production competing with one another, and finding customers in the bazaar. … The late Colonel Baird Smith estimated that about two-thirds of the population of India were clothed with indigenous cotton manufactures. Such a calculation was then only conjectural, nor could it be rendered with much greater accuracy now. We can only conclude, as a matter of general observation, that the native fabrics are slowly but surely giving place to the products of British industry.[25]

The prominence of Bombay for the Turkey red industry was a function of geography and the city's historical evolution under East India Company rule. As an island-based port facing west, it had natural advantages in trade with the Middle East and Africa and was the first point of contact for Europeans travelling overland from the Mediterranean via Alexandria and Aden (as taken by Matheson and his party in 1861) or later via the Suez Canal. Bombay had a cosmopolitan commercial community, with large numbers of Parsee businessmen who were widely respected in European trading circles; it had also evolved a system of British-owned commission agency houses for conducting trade and repatriating profits via bills of exchange drawn on partner firms in London[26] [Fig. 5.9]. The same system operated in Calcutta and Madras, and in the early nineteenth century the three cities were equal in importance, but Madras declined from the 1830s while Bombay, now Mumbai, flourished, exceeding Calcutta in relative importance and size during the cotton boom of the 1860s. Bombay was later eclipsed in size and importance by Calcutta, which had a growing export trade to East Asia, but retained a dominance of incoming goods from Europe.[27]

Yet, for all its vibrancy and opportunity, the Indian market was hard to regulate, with fraud, copyright infringement and difficulties in quality control frequently encountered. Business partnerships were easy to establish with some ethnic and religious groups, such as the Bombay Parsees, but not with others, and competing against local producers was always difficult [Fig. 5.10]. Indian taste was conservative and the best-valued textiles were always those produced by high-quality handcraft techniques. Despite Matheson's optimism about the demise of local industry in the face of imports, the wide availability in India of cheap synthetic red dyes from the 1880s, along with the expansion of local factory production for the mass market and also

Figure 5.9

Photograph showing a street in the commercial Fort area of Bombay, taken in the 1860s. The city was a major port and manufacturing centre, and a key component in the global trade of the Scottish Turkey red industry. By an unknown photographer, 1860s.

© The British Library Board

Figure 5.10

Hindu merchants from Delhi examining bolts of printed cloth imported from England. From John Forbes Watson's *The People of India* (1869), vol. 4, image 201.

Courtesy of Edinburgh University Library, ref: S.B.F572(54) Wat

for export to other parts of Asia and Africa, inevitably undermined the Turkey red industry in Scotland. A successful court case in Cawnpore in 1889, brought by the agents acting for the three Scottish Turkey red firms along with F. Steiner of Manchester, underlined the problem.

> It appeared when the matter was looked into that native-dyed grey cottons were being passed off by wholesale as European manufactured Turkey-red cloth. The dye used was found to be of German manufacture, imported in large quantities into Bombay under the name of alizarin, and with this a material was produced, which is described as exceedingly hard to distinguish from the genuine article. To the pieces of cloth thus manipulated forged European labels were deftly affixed, and the trade was pushed merrily along.[28]

Unlike Dundee's jute entrepreneurs, or some of the plain cotton masters of Glasgow, including John Muir of James Findlay & Co., Scottish Turkey red manufacturers seem to have made no efforts to invest in Indian production, or to diversify into other local manufactures or trades, such as tea dealing, though one entrepreneur, John Orr Ewing, did have financial interests in shipping companies in the East. With such high investments in design and dyeing and printing technologies at home, the Turkey red companies opted instead to maintain their core interest, to try to develop other eastern markets and cultivate domestic sales. The formation of the merged United Turkey Red Co. in 1898 was mainly to bring control to overseas markets and to India in particular. Unfortunately it was just too late, as the end of Empire, along with industrial transformation in Asia eventually spelled the end of the British cotton industry, including Turkey red.

East Asia, Africa and Australia

Writing from Singapore in 1854, the naturalist Alfred Russel Wallace was struck by the cosmopolitan character of the population that lived there, and observed that 'in costume these several peoples are as varied as in their speech'. These variations were significant in shaping British textile markets in South East Asia and beyond.

> The English preserve the tight fitting coat, waistcoat, and trowsers, and the abominable hat and cravat; the Portuguese patronise a light jacket, or more frequently shirt and trowsers only; the Malays wear their national jacket and sarong, with loose drawers; while the Chinese never depart in the least from their national dress, which, indeed, it is impossible to improve for a tropical climate, whether regards comfort or appearance. The loosely hanging trowsers, and neat white half-shirt half-jacket, is exactly what a dress should be in this latitude.[29]

India dominated Turkey red exports, but the qualities that made these cottons so popular in India – the bright colour-fast dyes and innovative designs – also appealed in other export markets such as Singapore, where local production using traditional craft techniques could not reproduce the same bold colours or consistent quality. Account book evidence for the firm of William Stirling & Sons in 1885, shows a range of eastern trading partners beyond India. The most important firm after Yule & Co. of Calcutta was Forrester & Co. of Shanghai, who mainly dealt in plain red cotton for further processing locally using the same bleaching and overprinting technique that was seen in India.[30] Other firms that dealt in Stirling's cottons were based in Batavia (now called Jakarta, capital of Java), Singapore, Manila, Colombo, Rangoon, Semarang, Macassar, Sura-baya and Hvilo.

Far-eastern markets were developed from Bombay or Calcutta, with many of the commission agents who dealt with firms like William Stirling & Sons in the 1850s and 1860s, chartering ships for trade to Shanghai and Singapore.[31] Access to the eastern trade also came directly from British ports, and the Museum's Turkey Red Collection includes a remarkable small volume, known as the Shanghai Pattern Book, which belonged to John Orr Ewing & Co.

for the period from December 1863 to October 1866, coinciding with the early development of the China trade. The volume, which includes only a limited range of patterned samples, all floral prints in a western style, along with plain Turkey red calicos, details a series of small consignments exported principally from Liverpool or Glasgow, with a few from London. All of these took advantage of newly-formed 'tea clipper' shipping lines, involving several famous high performance sailing vessels that were built in Glasgow.

The first consignment, of 14 December 1863, was on the *Pegasus* out of London, which was destined for China, possibly with the intention of returning with tea and also raw cotton, since this was at the height of the cotton famine arising from the American Civil War. The second consignment of 26 January 1864, from Liverpool, was on the famous racing clipper *Wild Deer*, which had been launched just a few months before at the Connell yard in Glasgow [Fig. 5.11]. It was mainly engaged in the tea trade between Shanghai and London, but carried a wide range of cargo and passengers on the outward journeys. By the 1870s, when the opening of the Suez Canal and advances in steam ships had superseded the ocean-going sailing clippers, the *Wild Deer*, in common with many similar ships, had switched to carrying emigrant passengers bound for Australia and New Zealand. It was wrecked off the coast of Ireland in January 1883, with a

Figure 5.11

The Shanghai Pattern Book details shipments of printed and plain Turkey red fabrics bound for Shanghai on tea clippers. John Orr Ewing & Co., 1863–66.

Paper and cotton; height 484 mm; width 590 mm

National Museums Scotland A.1962.1266.75.1.P3

general cargo of 900 tons from Glasgow and 209 passengers boarded at Greenock. All passengers and crew were saved.[32]

The maiden voyages of two ships built by Scotts & Co. of Greenock, which were the first of the famous Blue Funnel Line, the *Ajax* and the *Achilles*, contained Turkey red goods shipped by John Orr Ewing & Co. The voyages of *Ajax* are recorded in the journal of the ship's captain, Alexander Kidd, giving an insight into how trade was conducted by British entrepreneurs in a newly emerging market.

> July 1st 1866 commenced my first China voyage in the S.S. *Ajax* and made a very favourable passage direct to Mauritius. We had a small cargo and some 5 passengers, one too many a clergyman who took offence at a trifle and made himself generally disagreeable but he had the worst of it, a shallow vain fool and not much of the Christian about him, so far as I could see. I met some nice people in the Mauritius but had not much time with them as we were only two days there and off again for Penang (our next port). I had a good passage to Penang where we loaded some cargo and took a lot of Chinese deck passengers for Hong Kong and proceeded on to Singapore, discharged cargo from Lpool and filled up with local freight and passengers and started for Hong Kong and after a good run up the China sea arrd [arrived] in Hong Kong all well. Remained 5 days there, finished our work and started for Shanghai, had a fairly good passage & arrd in Shanghai Thursday Septr 20 1866.

> We stayed a month in Shanghai waiting to see if times would mend but found things getting no better. Started on the return journey with very little cargo and poor prospects. Still I had faith in something turning up. We took all we could get at Hong Kong & Singapore & Penang and we left Mauritius with 2000 tons space filled up. I was rather puzzled what to do with a fine ship going home 1/3 full not very promising for our new trade. But when approaching Algoa Bay I thought I would call at Port Elizabeth & try if I could get any cargo there, fortunately I did. We filled all our space with wool at a very fair rate & thus enabled me to finish my first China voyage very favourably.[33]

The last entry in the Shanghai Pattern Book is for 3 October 1866 and records a consignment sent on another famous ship, the *Fiery Cross*, which sailed in the Great Tea Race of 1866 and was owned by John M. Campbell & Sons of Glasgow, ship owners, ship and insurance brokers and export merchants. The Great Tea Race took place in spring and summer 1866, with the *Fiery Cross* racing against nine other ships from Shanghai to London, each laden with about one million pounds of tea. The ship's next journey eastwards carried John Orr Ewing's goods and with this consignment the Shanghai Pattern Book ends, though exports did continue, of course, with high expectations of riches to be made.

Yet despite expectations, the Far East market was difficult to penetrate, involving the British state in wars and gunboat diplomacy for decades. Indeed, some of the countries concerned, such as Java, were part of the empire possessions of other European nations, in this case the Dutch, who had settled there in large numbers since the seventeenth century. Much British trade in the east was of commodities produced in India, such as salt and, infamously, opium, which made vast profits for transport firms like Scottish-owned Jardine Matheson. China was particularly difficult and operated punitive local taxes on foreign traders, while Japan was largely closed to westerners until the 1870s. There were hopes that access to these markets would provide untold opportunities for British entrepreneurs and manufacturers, as well as acting as a source of raw materials for return to Britain. But China and Japan were different to India, better able to develop their own modern textile industries, with Japan soon coming to dominate Asian textile production. Moreover, the people of these countries, which were colder than India, were not so reliant on cotton for their clothing. In the event, though trade became easier as a string of free ports were established across Asia, the demand for British cotton in countries that already had their own sophisticated textile traditions in wool and silk as well as cotton remained relatively low. At its high-point in the mid-1890s, China accounted for just ten per cent of British cotton exports,[34] while British imports from China were dominated by tea and fine silk, much as it had been a century before. By the end of the 1890s the China market was proving so difficult for Scotland's United Turkey Red Co. that a decision was made that no more goods be shipped there and China production was suspended until trading conditions had improved.[35]

Turkey red exports to China and Japan were mainly of plain dyed cottons and yarns. Patterned goods were, however, made for the Indonesian market where they were used for making sarongs, which were worn by both men and women, by natives and also by some European settlers. Alfred Russel Wallace offers an insight:

> The 'sarong' is a curious garment; it is a ring or cylinder of calico, about a yard deep and a yard and a half in diameter; it is worn in all sorts of ways; either over one shoulder as a scarf, or wrapped round

the body like a Scotch plaid, or more generally put round the waist like a petticoat, and twisted or tucked in a great bunch in front, having a curious and uncomfortable appearance, though, for its being generally of bright colours, it is not unpicturesque.[36]

Visitors to Indonesia, including Wallace, were struck by the fact that Dutch settlers wore the sarong.

The manners and customs of the Dutch are certainly curious. A Dutch lady does not dress until late in the afternoon, but wears from early morning a light robe called a sarong, a short morning jacket and a pair of slippers .... Though made of sea cotton only, [the sarongs] are hand painted in quaint designs and colours, blue and brown predominating, by the natives of Central Java and fetch very high prices .... Each Dutch lady owns several, of which she is very proud .... Both ladies and gentlemen sit until late in the day in *deshebille*, the former as above described, the latter in pyjamas made from a sarong and a light shirt.[37]

Sarong patterns can be seen throughout the Turkey Red Collection, including imitations of traditional batik designs, which were often highly symbolic in character [Figs 5.12 and 5.13]. Since the Indonesian population was largely Islamic by the nineteenth century, designs for this market tended toward the abstract or geometric, with floral motifs more commonly observed than animal or human figures. Indonesian patterns were much larger than those typically designed for the Indian market, and involve fewer colours. Large patterns historically had been associated with the royal family and with important court officials, and some patterns were also traditionally exclusive to the élite. Although strict dress regulation had waned by the nineteenth century, these conventions still influenced local fashions and demands.[38] That the Indonesian market was important for the Scottish Turkey red industry is indicated on the formation of the United Turkey Red Co. in 1898, when decisions were made to cut some areas of production and dispose of many print plates. A 'Valuation Committee' reported that

[all] calico printing stocks, as opposed to Turkey Red Prints, are rejected, as not being advantageous to the business of the United Turkey Red Co. Ltd, with the exception of Red & Yellow Scarves, Black ground garments & scarves, by Cylinder or Block, & what is known as Batick styles.[39]

Figure 5.12 (right)

A sample of flat press printed cotton cloth. This is a sarong design with large floral motifs in the centre, trailing vines in triangles, and a floral border. It was probably produced for the Indonesian market. Archibald Orr Ewing & Co., May 1883.

Cotton; height 490mm; width 306mm

National Museums Scotland
A.1962.1266.8.1.309

Figure 5.13 (below)

The Indonesian market continued to be important to the Scottish Turkey red industry into the 20th century. These samples are from a pattern book entitled 'Sarongs and Slandangs' which dates from 1912. United Turkey Red Co. Ltd, 1912.

Cotton; height 76mm; width 151mm

National Museums Scotland
A.1962.1266.31.15.387

Indonesian demand was large but also intensely competitive, as indicated in a letter sent to John Orr Ewing & Co. from C. H. Eccles, a Manchester clerk seeking employment:

> I trust you will excuse the liberty I take in addressing you, but knowing your esteemed Firm to be largely interested in the Java markets, I respectfully beg to offer my services …. For the past 10 years I have had the entire management of the Java Consignment Department of

> Messrs. F. Steiner & Co. Ltd of Church [near Manchester], during which period, as you are doubtless well aware, their business with the Java Markets especially Batavia and Sourabya, has enormously increased. Under these circumstances I need hardly say that I am thoroughly conversant with the requirements etc of the said Markets & I flatter myself that you could put my services to considerable profit.[40]

Mr Eccles was not hired. A couple of years later, the head of UTR's Manchester office, William Hood, when writing to the shipping yarn department in Glasgow, gave another insight into the Indonesian market as he sought to 're-open a business in yarns for Manilla' through specialist London agent, Albert Coates & Co.

> For some time the business has been done from Barcelona, mainly for Turkey Red, and the counts were 16' from 30' and 22' from 40'. Mr Coates suggests two consignment lots, one to their old clients, and one to a new and rich firm, which has recently been asking for Try Red yarns. He further suggests two bales to each House, – one of the low counts and one of the high. Of course, Mr Coates cannot now say whether these firms would accept such lots as 'consignments', or only sell on Coates' A/C. In any case, Mr Coates would assure us of payment.[41]

Though the far-eastern trade was problematical for Scotland's Turkey red manufacturers, Chinese and other eastern-styled patterns are seen frequently in the Museum's patterns books, often showing human figures such as children at play or traditional warriors [Fig. 5.14]. But these designs were not necessarily for export. Britain was familiar with Chinese motifs from the long-established porcelain trade and fashion for Chinoiserie, and there was a strong Victorian interest in Chinese decorative arts and fine embroidered silks. It seems likely, therefore, that quasi-Chinese styles may well have been consumed in Britain. Similarly, the interest in Japanese design, which was stimulated by a swift opening of Japanese trading connections from the 1870s as well as the import of fine Japanese textiles and crafts, influenced British art and design more generally and can be seen in some Turkey red patterns for consumption at home [Fig. 5.15].

Developing alongside the Asian markets, trade with north Africa and Egypt was greatly enhanced by the opening of the Suez Canal in 1869, and was fuelled by Britain's considerable political interests in the Middle East. Scottish Turkey red producers made commemo-

Figure 5.14

Design of a samurai on a red ground, painted on paper and intended for printed cotton. It is thought that this design was intended for western markets. John Orr Ewing & Co., 1870s–1880s.

Paper; height 480 mm; width 490 mm

National Museums Scotland A.1962.1266.27.1.4826

Figure 5.15

Sample of cylinder printed cotton cloth with a white stencil style design of a building, waves and East Asian writing. John Orr Ewing & Co., late 19th century.

Cotton; height 122 mm; width 270 mm

National Museums Scotland A.1962.1266.10.5.4930

rative handkerchiefs to celebrate some of the key events associated with growing British links with this region; and a number of designs, which can be dated to the later nineteenth century, show Arabic scenes, with camels and the common use of the Islamic Red Crescent device [Figs 5.16 and 5.17; see also Fig. 4.37]. Whether these were for sale in Britain or in Turkey and the Middle East is unclear, but certainly by the 1870s Britain had a robust trade in many commodities with the eastern Mediterranean area that was known as the Levant. Indeed the Levant was as important an export market for British-made cottons as China in the late nineteenth century[42]; and though business records are few, we know that Archibald Orr Ewing & Co. exported to Greece, Iran and Iraq in the 1890s.[43]

British trade with sub-Saharan Africa was slow to develop, and much of that market, particularly in eastern and southern Africa, was supplied from India through networks of Indian businessmen who migrated to countries like Kenya. The town-based Indian populations in Africa were big purchasers of imported cottons, but as a relatively expensive commodity the native African market for Turkey red prints

Figure 5.16

Textile design of a camel wearing a harness and saddle with tassels. Crescent moon and star motifs are placed around the edges of the circle. The design was painted onto paper and intended for cylinder printed cottons. From a pattern book thought to have belonged to William Stirling & Sons, late 19th century.

Paper; height 665 mm; width 660 mm

National Museums Scotland
A.1962.1266.28.2.2993

Figure 5.17

Textile design depicting a man in Middle Eastern military uniform and crescent moon and star motifs. The figure bears a resemblance to Abbas II who became the last Khedive of Egypt in 1892 and it is possible the design was produced to commemorate this occasion. The design was painted onto paper and intended for cylinder printed cottons. From a pattern book thought to have belonged to William Stirling & Sons, c.1892.

Paper; height 400 mm; width 310 mm

National Museums Scotland
A.1962.1266.28.2.3438

was always limited. However, African locals did consume bandanna and handkerchief exports, although not necessarily through purchase. A newspaper report of 1885, detailing a temperance demonstration in Greenock, describes how the speaker displayed two examples of Turkey red pocket-handkerchiefs that were manufactured in Glasgow for sending to Africa. Both were printed with beer bottles and the name of a famous local brewer, and had been shipped in vast numbers as a form of advertising for the brewer involved.[44]

Perhaps the most famous Turkey red artefact associated with Africa is the iconic plain red shirt that was owned and worn by missionary, explorer and anti-slavery campaigner Dr David Livingstone, which has survived among his personal possessions in the David Livingstone Centre in Blantyre. African-styled garments are noted in some early twentieth-century pattern books; they were described as 'khangas', a type of sarong worn in East Africa. While the sales book maintained by Archibald Orr Ewing & Co. between 1895 and 1898 records orders sent to Capetown and Natal, both in South Africa, British colonial consignments also included Australasia, with goods shipped to Brisbane, Auckland, Sydney, Wellington and Adelaide.[45]

Both South Africa and Australia, with their large British emigrant populations, consumed similar styles and patterns to those sold in Britain. The Australian market was particularly connected with the activities of the firm of John Orr Ewing, who invested heavily in the 1850s and 1860s in the European and Australian Royal Mail Company, which ran a postal, passenger and goods service via Suez and Ceylon to Melbourne and Sydney.[46] Turkey red goods were advertised in the press from the early nineteenth century, when convict transportation and penal settlement still operated. John McLeod, who was a storekeeper at the Elizabeth River near Campbelltown in Tasmania, specified a stock of 'Monteith's Turkey red bandannas' in an advert of 1827, with Monteith's famous branded goods advertised widely by numerous retail outlets, many owned by Scots, in the decades that followed.[47]

In the 1830s, the Australian female market began to appear, with newspaper adverts for 'Turkey red shawls with chintz borders'[48] and 'twilled Turkey red cotton for ladies and children's dresses'.[49] The idea of specific local markets within the region was also indicated, as in 1844 with an advertisement by Rowan, McNab & Co. of Sydney for 'Turkey red prints, showy patterns' and 'Turkey red handkerchiefs, showy patterns' that stated that these 'have been imported expressly for the New Zealand and South Sea trade'[50] [see Fig. 5.18 and Fig. 5.18]. The South Sea trade, as with the trade with the local Aboriginal populations, was

Figure 5.18

Engraving showing the traditional male costume of Tahiti at the end of the 19th century. There are clear similarities in the cloth pattern of the sarong or pareo on the left with those in the Turkey Red Collection. An engraving, 1880.

© De Agostini/British Library Board

Figure 5.19

Sample of Turkey red dyed cotton with a lead plate printed 'motif and stripe' design with a stylised exotic flower motif and a stripe with geometric shapes at the side. This design could have been for the South Pacific market where the motif and stripe combination was used in sarongs. John Orr Ewing & Co., c.1873–95.

Cotton; height 430 mm; width 550 mm

National Museums Scotland A.1962.1266.12.10.1420

mainly by barter. It involved tobacco, beads, and pieces of brightly coloured Turkey red cotton which were exchanged for exotic animal skins and native artefacts that found a ready market as curios for domestic decoration, and supplying the growing numbers of British museum collections.[51] One widely reported expedition was that undertaken by Henry Chester, a police magistrate from Thursday Island, Queensland, who was charged with establishing friendly relations with the people of the Maicussar River area in New Guinea. This he did with gifts of trinkets and Turkey red.[52] Turkey red textiles had great status value among the native peoples and certainly made a visual impact. A visitor to the South Sea island of Aoba described the local pilot who helped to navigate a difficult river as dressed in nothing but a primitive loin cloth and a European 'stove pipe' hat embellished with yards of Turkey red wrapped around the crown and cascading down behind.[53]

Australia was still an important market in the late nineteenth century, but that country, like so many others with British connections, also imported cotton goods from other producers such as India and Japan. Moreover, much as in North America, there were telling moves to establish an indigenous cotton dyeing and printing industry. In 1855, the textile firm of John Ross & Co. of Melbourne advertised 'Wanted, a Turkey red dyer'.[54] Whether they found a suitable candidate locally, or from among the numerous Scottish emigrants that flocked to Australia from the 1850s, is not recorded.

Notes

1. D. A. Farnie, *The English Cotton Industry and the World Market 1815–1896* (Oxford, 1979), ch 3.
2. *Penny Magazine of the Society for the Diffusion of Useful Knowledge*, 27 July 1844, p. 289.
3. *New York Gazette*, 17 September 1810.
4. Mary Schoeser, 'Of clans, kirks, cows and calico' in Liz Arthur (ed.) *Seeing Red: Scotland's Exotic Textile Heritage* (Glasgow, 2007) p. 18.
5. Andrew Ure, 'Description of the Great Bandana Gallery in the Turkey red factory of Messrs Monteith and Co. at Glasgow', *The Glasgow Mechanics' Magazine and Annals of Philosophy* (Glasgow, 1831), pp.7–10.
6. *New York Gazette*, 13 October 1797.
7. 'Dress under difficulties; or passages from the blockade experience of rebel women', *Godey's Lady's Book and Magazine* (July, 1866), pp. 32–33.
8. W. A. Cooper, 'Artists in their studios: Daniel

8. C. Beard', *Godey's Magazine* (August, 1895), p. 177.
9. TNA: BT44/23, Register 1863–69 and BT43/292 registered design number 177416.
10. See Robert Bishop, *Folk Painters of America* (New York, 1979) p. 11.
11. *Godey's Magazine* (September, 1896), p. 321.
12. *Godey's Magazine* (June, 1897), p. 660.
13. *Maine Farmer*, 10 July 1884.
14. Barbara Brackman, *Clues in the Calico: A Guide to Identifying and Dating Antique Quilts* (Lafayette, CA, 2009), p. 63.
15. See, for example, 'Location, soil and cultivation of the madder crop', *The New York Farmer*, 3 March 1837.
16. The others were: Merrimack Printworks, Massachusetts; Little Falls Dye Works and Bleachery, New Jersey; Times Dyeing and Finishing Works, Pennsylvania; and the Turkey Red Co. in Rhode Island, *Textile Manufacturer's Directory of the United States and Canada* (New York, 1887).
17. *History of the State of Rhode Island and Providence Plantations* (New York, 1920), 'Biographical', pp. 195–96.
18. UGA: UGD 13/5/1. Home sales book, William Stirling & Sons, 1895.
19. Farnie, *English Cotton Industry*, p. 101.
20. National Museums Scotland: Turkey Red Collection. Accession no. A.1962.1266.31.6.
21. See Ch. 1 for details of Matheson's career.
22. Matheson, *England to Delhi*.
23. J. Forbes Munro, *Maritime Enterprise and Empire: Sir William Mackinnon and his Business* (Woodbridge, 2003), pp. 43–53
24. Matheson, *England to Delhi*, pp. 400–1.
25. Ibid, pp. 359–60.
26. Anthony Webster, 'The strategies and limits of gentlemanly capitalism: the London East India agency houses, provincial commercial interests, and the evolution of British economic policy in South and South East Asia, 1800–50', *Economic History Review*, 59:4 (2006), pp. 743–64.
27. Claude Markovits, *Merchants, Traders, Entrepreneurs: Indian Business in the Colonial Era* (Basingstoke, 2008).
28. *Times of India*, 28 August 1889.
29. Alfred Russel Wallace, Letter dated 26 September 1854, *The Literary Gazette and Journal of Belles Lettres*. [Accessed online 22/03/2013]
30. UGA: UGD 13/3/1 William Stirling & Sons. Private Ledger, 1881-85.
31. See, *The Bombay Times and Journal of Commerce*, 17 January 1855. 'Vessels in Harbour', which note ships chartered by Grey & Co., Huschke & Co. and Frith & Co., who all placed orders with Stirlings.
32. *Glasgow Herald*, 6 February 1883.
33. Mersey Maritime Museum, Liverpool. MS, 'Jottings from a Sailor's Life. The Journal of Alexander Kidd'. [Accessed online 22/03/2013]
34. Farnie, *English Cotton Industry*, p. 91.
35. MCRO: UTR Minute Book no. 2, 4 July 1900.
36. Wallace, letter dated October 10, 1854. [Accessed online 22 March 2013]
37. *Times of India*, 29 May 1884.
38. See, Australian Museum website 'The Batik Process' at: http://australianmuseum.net.au/The-Batik-Process
39. MCRO: UTR Minute Book no. 1. 27 April 1898.
40. UGA: UGD 13/5/13/4/11. Letter dated 26 September 1899 in bundle dated 1898–99.
41. UGA: UGD13/5/13/2/12. Memorandum 2, dated December 1901.
42. Farnie, *English Cotton Industry*, p. 91.
43. UGA: UGD13/5/2. Archibald Orr Ewing & Co. Sales Book, 1895–98.
44. *Glasgow Herald*, 21 September 1885.
45. UGA: UGD13/5/2. Archibald Orr Ewing & Co. Sales Book, 1895–98.
46. *Sydney Morning Herald,* 23 September 1856.
47. *Colonial Times and Tasmanian Advertiser*, 9 February 1827.
48. *Sydney Gazette and New South Wales Advertiser*, 15 July 1830.
49. *Sydney Herald*, 18 August 1834.
50. *Sydney Morning Herald*, 14 February 1844.
51. 'Among the objects added to the Museum [of the Society of Antiquaries] by purchase during the year are a large assortment of weapons from Australia and the South Sea Islands', *Scotsman*, 2 December 1869.
52. Henry M. Chester, *Narrative of Expeditions to New Guinea in a Series of Letters* (Brisbane, 1878), pp. 5–6.
53. *South Australian Register*, 17 February 1885.
54. *Argus*, 20 December 1855.

CHAPTER SIX

Home markets

TURKEY RED manufacturers had always sold some of their output in Britain, and as export markets came under pressure the development of new fabrics and designs for domestic consumption increased. Turkey red textiles were a luxury for many, but the market grew with rising living standards and new aspirations for domestic comfort. The dark red colour schemes favoured by Victorian householders, created by the wealthy using costly velvets and damask, were made possible for the middle and for the working classes through curtains, upholstery or bed covers in Turkey red cottons in imitation styles.

Turkey red cotton was used for home-made clothing, particularly for children, and could be purchased from remnant warehouses such as Bannerman's on Lothian Street in Edinburgh who, throughout the 1860s, advertised Turkey red prints for sale along with fancy tartans and colourful flannels. Discounted factory sales, often following the frequent fires that beset the cotton printing industry, as at William Stirling & Sons' Cordale Works in August 1889, brought large quantities of fabrics that were mainly intended for export, and therefore of exotic designs, into the homes of ordinary Scots for clothing or furnishings.[1] Turkey red was also used for ready-made clothing, particularly quilted garments as advertised in the *Scotsman* on 5 October 1865 by Misses Fairgrieve's Millinery, Corset and Crinoline Warehouse of Princes Street, Edinburgh. Here, as elsewhere, the marketing emphasis was on the capacity for Turkey red prints to look more luxurious than they were, while still being practical and washable.

> Misses Fairgrieve have just received a large supply of Booth & Fox's justly celebrated eider duck and arctic goose down clothing, which is now in very great demand. Real down under and over skirts, dress improvers, quilts, dressing gowns, vests, chest protectors etc, which are much warmer than flannel and not half the weight. A sure protection again an easterly wind. Most of them are covered in fast

Opposite page:

An example of 'two red' colouring, sometimes likened to more expensive damask (see Fig. 6.4).

National Museums Scotland

coloured Turkey red chintz patterns which are equal in effect to rich Indian shawls and can be washed with the down inside.

Clothing and home dressmaking

Whole dresses in Turkey red prints were commonly made and fashionable in the early decades of the nineteenth century, with several examples surviving in museum collections such as Platt Hall in Manchester [Fig. 6.1]. Portraits from this period sometimes show colourful printed dresses and shawls that were probably made out of these then relatively scarce and expensive vibrant textiles. Turkey red working shirts for men were also manufactured, the most famous survival being that owned mid-century by David Livingstone on his travels in Africa, and which he was reputedly wearing when he met Henry Stanley. The shirt, which is styled like a loose, collar-less smock, has prominent white stitching on the front and is displayed today at the David Livingstone Centre in Lanarkshire.

Figure 6.1

Dress made of Turkey red dyed and printed cotton, 1820–1830.

© Manchester City Galleries

At a time when the woven or printed Paisley shawl was still fashionable, Scotland produced and exported large quantities of printed cotton shawls with fringes. An auction of damaged piece goods in Glasgow in 1845 comprised thousands of such shawls in Turkey red and yellow or white, as well as 'Swiss fancy shawls', which were saved from the barque *Valpariaso*, which had been wrecked on a voyage from Liverpool to South America.[2] Some of these shawls would have been sold on to local consumers in Britain, but as shawls went out of fashion and the Turkey red industry increased production for export, the fashionable status at home was undermined. By mid-century the taste for very bright colours in women's fashionable clothing had ended, replaced by black and muted shades reflecting the 'seriousness' of the age, as well as the new availability of good black logwood dyes or such subtle new colours as mauve, which was the product of innovations in dyeing technology.[3] Turkey red fabric only really survived in high-cost manufactured clothing where the relative value of the garment was enhanced by other processes and materials, such as the McLintock's quilted down petticoats which are described later in this chapter. It also remained in use for underclothes, because it was colour fast and could therefore be worn next to the skin.

By the second half of the century, manufactured ready-made clothing in Turkey red was mostly for practical wear, such as aprons, or was for children where durability and frequent washing qualities had an obvious appeal. An example is furnished by the Glasgow drapers Copland & Lye in Cowcaddens, who advertised a 'manufacturer's stock of Turkey red apron pinafores, handsomely embroidered' that originally sold for 8s 6d a piece and was now discounted to 3s 6d.[4] One of the more unusual lines of children's garments to be made was one-piece bathing dresses for boys and girls, where the market was among the middle classes or those prosperous families of the labouring élite who could now afford an annual seaside holiday. Examples of such garments, which were trimmed with white braid or tape, and sometimes also included detachable skirts for girls, have survived in the Bethnal Green Museum of Childhood in London. Several of these swimsuits include labels stating the manufacturer's name – United Turkey Red, which places the date of manufacture to the years following the industry merger in 1898 – with the declaration 'Genuine Turkey Red' and, in one case, a retail price of 1s 9½d.[5]

Printed handkerchiefs and bandannas were an export staple and were produced in millions throughout the life of the industry. They were also, of course, consumed at home, and, because they were so cheap, sometimes they were given away as a marketing gimmick, as in 1853 when the Christmas promotion of ready-made dresses, hosiery and drapery at Philip & Kennedy of Union Buildings, Aberdeen, included the statement:

> Every purchaser to the extent of 5s will be presented with a TURKEY RED HANDKERCHIEF, FREE.[6]

The Bombay Pattern Book, which was maintained by William Stirling & Sons between 1853 and 1868, provides several examples of handkerchiefs for copying, along with detailed orders for sizes, designs and quantities required. For instance, in a letter dated 25 February 1857, Grey & Co. commission agents in Bombay requested 'an assortment of Turkey red print handkerchiefs, previous muster 23 x 28 inches, but would prefer 25 inches square'. The order comprised 150 cases with half of the handkerchiefs in red and pink, a third of the content in red and green, and the remainder in red and blue.[7] The styles seen here for sale in Bombay, which increasingly made use of western decorative motifs, would also have been sold at home in Britain [Fig. 6.2].

Figure 6.2

The green and red handkerchief design at the bottom of this image, which would not have looked out of place in the British market, was requested by agents of William Stirling & Sons in 1857 for sale in India.

Paper and cotton; height 510 mm; width 330 mm

National Museums Scotland A.1962.1266.31.6.P35

The handkerchiefs exported to India were used as scarves or head coverings, or for carrying babies in a sling, and even for wrapping goods for travelling. They were used for similar purposes in Europe too, particularly among peasant populations that still favoured bright and gaudy colours, as a Scottish newspaper travel account of a trip to Galicia and Coruna in Spain 1891 revealed. The author described the clothing of the 'market women' as a blaze of colour with Turkey red handkerchiefs with large patterns particularly prominent. The biggest of these handkerchiefs were worn over the shoulders and across the bosom, covering part of the 'chemise' or short gown, before being crossed to the back and tied with a knot.[8]

Another prominent use of handkerchiefs by peasant women was noted on the Isle of St Kilda, again as described by a traveller, who related how, having endured over eight months of isolation due to bad weather, the St Kildans came out in celebration in June 1886 to greet the first ship to make landfall with news and supplies. The men were dressed in heavy garments made of blanketing and were 'muffled' up to their ears in big coarse cravats twisted round their necks, 'roll after roll'. The women, however, 'made a much more picturesque group'. They were barefoot, with short petticoats and dresses to their knees, and for head-dresses they 'disported' bright Turkey red napkins which, according to report, were worn at all times.[9] Photographs for the period survive, of course, and certainly show the St Kildan women in head scarves, but, being black and white, it is impossible to tell if they were Turkey red cotton or some other textile [Fig. 6.3].

Scotland's ordinary working classes wore Turkey red handkerchiefs. Male factory hands in the Vale of Leven wound them around the neck as work-wear for mopping up their sweat, and working-class women often wore them as decorative scarves and shawls. The latter is evident from a newspaper description of an unidentified corpse that was removed from the River Clyde in the autumn of 1846. The woman, estimated to be in her forties, was comfortably dressed in the working-class fashion in a lilac printed bed-gown, black and blue striped drugget petticoat, Turkey red handkerchief, grey worsted stockings, carpet shoes and a blue striped cotton apron.[10]

Drapers, such as Copland & Lye of Glasgow, sold boys' Turkey red handkerchiefs, 'just the thing for school' and handkerchiefs for ladies, all at 1s per dozen.[11] Handkerchiefs also featured in the royal trousseau for Princess Victoria Melitia's wedding in 1894, including dozens in fine white cambric with coloured borders in pale blue, mauve, pink, green and alternate squares of white and Turkey red.[12] Princess Victoria Melitia was the eldest daughter of the then Duke of Edinburgh, which probably accounts for the Turkey red accents in the trousseau and the detailed newspaper reports in Scotland. She was Queen Victoria's granddaughter.

Turkey red handkerchiefs or bandannas had many uses, and these versatile items could be used for celebration, advertising and promotions as well as clothing. The Scottish manufacturers produced beautifully designed commemorative handkerchiefs for numerous occasions at home and abroad, some of them surviving in the Museum's Turkey

Figure 6.3

This photograph of women of St Kilda was taken in the early 20th century. The woman in the foreground is wearing a printed shawl with paisley shapes, which could easily be Turkey red dyed and printed cotton. Photograph taken by Michael Stevenson, 1913.

© National Records of Scotland [GD1/713/1/7]

Red Collection, such as the handkerchiefs to mark the end of the Crimea War that included portraits of Scottish war heroes [See Fig. 4.34]. The best of these handkerchiefs were described in detail in the press, as with the one famously produced by William Stirling & Sons in 1851 to celebrate the Great Exhibition, which was sold in thousands as souvenirs. At a Temperance Demonstration held in Greenock in September 1885, one of the speakers, James Hamilton, 'in the course of a spirited address', produced two Turkey red pocket handkerchiefs that were printed with images of beer bottles and glasses and the name of a well-known Scottish brewer, and explained, with manifest contempt for corrupting commerce, that large numbers of these handkerchiefs were being manufactured in Glasgow as advertisements for beer.[13] Although the manufacturer is not named, it was almost certainly Henry Monteith & Co., a firm that finally ceased trading in 1888 after over a century in business, blaming 'dullness in trade' and depression in the eastern exchanges.[14] One similar example in the Museum's Turkey Red Collection, also from the 1880s, though not depicting beer, does show a wine or liquor carafe surrounded by glasses and cherries [See Fig. 4.42].

The home market for clothing made from Turkey red cotton was dominated by the simple handkerchief for much of the century, but the rise of home dressmaking considerably increased use of the fabric in domestic contexts. As living standards rose generally among the working classes, it was not unusual to find quantities of textiles in ordinary homes, for clothing and other uses too. An illustration is provided by the Glasgow novelist Sarah Tytler in her 1889 novel *A Houseful of Girls*, which gives an account of a group of young people who put on a theatrical entertainment to amuse their friends. Perhaps, not surprisingly, Turkey red cottons make a useful and showy effect.

> Annie and Dora had appeared in magnificent chintz sacques – which might have represented tea-gowns – and mob caps, and had been declared … a most satisfactory eighteenth century pair. Cyril … had figured in black satin trunk hose, velvet doublet, and lace collar of a Spanish grandee. But Ned Hewett had stuck to Turkey red cotton for a Venetian senator or a Roman cardinal, nobody had been quite certain which.[15]

Women had always made some of their own and their family's clothing by hand, but the introduction of the domestic sewing machine transformed this activity. Sewing machines were advertised widely for industrial use from the early 1850s, and were soon also available on the second-hand market. The impact was swift, though not always seen as positive, as revealed in an article in the *Spectator*, reproduced in the provincial press, titled 'Painless extinction of sempstresses'.[16] An essay on the same subject by Glasgow statistician Dr John Strang was presented to the meeting of the British Association in Leeds in September 1858, titled 'The sewing machine in Glasgow, and its effects on production, prices, and wages'. It revealed that the best sewing machines cost between £25 and £30 and there were estimated to be about 900 machines in Glasgow at that time. Although the undermining of handwork was evident, it was also stated that those who operated sewing machines were paid more than formerly for their hand-sewing.[17] With many patents registered, and the domestic market in sight, the late 1850s saw the introduction of a new type of lighter and cheaper sewing machine suitable for home use, such as the one produced by the British Sewing Machine Company, priced at £14, and described as 'the only family sewing machine made in Great Britain'. It was advertised from 1859 along with similar machines made by the American Singer Sewing Machine Company, which later established a factory at Clydebank near Glasgow, and the appeal was immediate.

> By and by, a sewing machine will be as essential an article of household furniture as a piano-forte. Its cheerful click will supply a much more useful kind of music, just sufficient, indeed – at least in the case of the British sewing machine – to lull any wakeful infant asleep, while the mother is plying her thrifty task.[18]

Home dressmaking was made quicker and easier with the birth of the sewing machine, but assembling the fabric pieces for sewing required cutting skills that were usually beyond the average housewife. In response to an emerging market, some enterprising businesswomen from the commercial dressmaking sector, who inevitably were seeing their own businesses undermined by the domestic sewing machine, would cut out materials in advance and sell them for sewing up at home.[19] They included 'Madame Levine' of 248 Sauchiehall Street in Glasgow, who advertised that she 'cuts, fits and artistically drapes ladies' own materials for home dressmaking; newest styles'.[20] Madam Levine gave classes in home dressmaking, as did several of her competitors, including Madame Bowman, the Misses Wilson and Mrs Young, who all offered a similar range of services and advertised in the same newspaper editions. Commercial paper patterns, dressmaking magazines likes *Weldon's Home Dressmaker*, which was first published in 1888, and published dress cutting-out systems, were also widely available by the end of the century. It was a boom time for domestic retail sales of fabrics, as shown in advertisements placed by the Glasgow departmental store of Pettigrew & Stephens.

> Dress goods … unparalleled selection. It would seem as if the Rodmure and other good systems of dress cutting were giving a great impetus to home dressmaking as not for years has so much good material been sold over the counter as during this season.[21]

Home dressmakers used a range of fabrics, but cotton was particularly popular because it was cheap to buy and easy to sew, giving a clean and professional-looking finish for those with modest skills. The choice available in shops was vast and frequent damage to consignments destined for the export market resulted in cut-price exotic-designed cottons also advertised for sale by local retailers, especially in Glasgow. One of these sales – arising from a salvage operation when the ship *William III* was sunk near Liverpool – was held in the famous Royal Polytechnic Warehouse in 1871. The newspaper advertisement detailed 3,500 yards of Turkey red cotton 'slightly damaged by salt water', which was a 'portion on a cargo intended for India' comprising small prints that were suitable for 'children's pinafores, frocks, ladies dresses, bed mats and a host of other purposes'.[22] Damaged goods like these were sold at about a quarter of the export price, for as little as 3d per yard, and were frequently advertised, as were the wholesale salvage auctions that provided retailers with their stock. Another notable Glasgow draper that often carried cut-price, damaged and bankrupt auction stock, Copland & Lye, advertised Turkey red cotton frills for sale in 1876, describing them as 'very fashionable for trimmings on skirts or morning wrappers'. The plain frills retailed at 3 1/4d per yard, and the patterns, sold in pieces of 12 yards, were 7s 11d and 9s 6d per piece.[23]

The availability of sewing machines and cheap textiles easily purchased through local drapers meant that housewives sometimes turned their attention to patchwork quilt-making, often using distinctive local or regional designs, with many examples surviving in local museums and also in the York collection of the Quilters' Guild.[24] The names of these domestic quilters are mostly long forgotten, but one unusual case is well documented. This is a large and spectacular quilt in the collections of the McManus Museum and Gallery in Dundee, which was made by Nicholas White of Dundee, a steward on a whaling ship in the late nineteenth century, whose quilt was constructed from over 100 differently designed textile samples, mostly in Turkey red, taken from manufacturer's pattern books. It is assumed that the quilting was done while White was at sea, and the design is one that was common in Scotland and Ireland at that time. How he acquired the pattern books is unknown, but perhaps, like the fabric that was purchased by female home dressmakers and quilters on land, they were also part of a sale of salvaged stock.

Furnishings

Britain in the late nineteenth century experienced a revolution in domestic comfort as rising living standards, the consequence of cheap food imports, generated surplus incomes for ordinary householders which were spent by many on home furnishings and decoration. The Turkey red textile manufacturers, keen to develop their domestic markets in the face of growing competition abroad, responded to this new demand by creating 'furniture' designs in muted 'tasteful' colours and patterns, and inventing new printing techniques that reproduced an impression of such expensive fabrics as satin damask or velvet. The Museum's Turkey Red Collection includes several pattern books containing furniture prints, including what are described as 'two red' furniture patterns. This refers to two shades of red in a single piece of fabric, which was achieved through a weak discharging solution applied in a pattern through two lead plates, to create a lighter shade of pink on the red ground. Typical designs for this sort of fabric included British woodland birds and floral motifs in imitation of designs made popular by famous designers like William Morris [Fig. 6.4].

Figure 6.4

The 'two red' colouring lent itself well to the furnishing fabrics produced by the Turkey red manufacturers in the late 19th century, and were sometimes likened to more expensive damask. From an unidentified Vale of Leven firm, late 19th century.

Cotton; height 436mm; width 279mm

National Museums Scotland A.1962.1266.20.1.3174

Figure 6.5

Patterns for furnishing fabrics tended to be larger and bolder than those intended for clothing. The 'two red' colouring was often overprinted with another colour – such as white, as seen here. Unidentified Vale of Leven firm, post 1876.

Cotton; height 495 mm; width 615 mm

National Museums Scotland A.1962.1266.21.1.3004

'Two reds' were sometimes used in patterns that incorporated white and yellow discharge printing, to represent well-loved flowers like lily-of-the-valley, and were sometimes over-printed with green or white detail [Fig. 6.5]. Glazed finishes, giving a sheen to fabric and protection from staining and wear, were also developed, in imitation of glazed chintz, again for the furnishings market [Fig. 6.6].

Victorian and Edwardian domestic interiors were increasingly complex and cluttered, with reds and dark colours particularly favoured and with a growing use of upholstery and cushions to render furniture comfortable.[25] The best front room, lovingly maintained by proud housewives, was a prominent feature of new suburban housing, and household guides for the later nineteenth century, which were aimed at the middle and working classes, put a stress on domestic hygiene through frequent washing and airing in sunlight. Turkey red cottons, with their fast dyes and easy drying qualities, were favoured for practicality as well as colour in the sitting room or bedroom. Highlighting this growing domestic market, the Glasgow drapers Copland & Lye were regular advertisers of Turkey red twills, describing

> … hundreds of pieces of this wonderful washing fabric, which is now being used for children's and ladies dresses, for underclothing for travelling and for covering furniture.[26]

They also regularly advertised 'soft' Turkey red cloth; this was for use as dusters.[27]

Details contained in a 'home sales' order book that has survived for William Stirling & Sons for 1895 shows orders of Turkey red fabric that were sent out to British retailers ranging from big departmental stores like Wylie & Lochhead of Buchanan Street in Glasgow or Marshall & Snelgrove in London, to local drapers like Henry Murty of Arbroath.[28] An 1886 catalogue for G. W. Harding's linen warehouse in York details 'Scotch' Turkey red table covers that are patterned with 'ferns and flowers' or in the 'Queen's household' style, made up in five different sizes, along with Turkey red damask for sale by the yard. A newspaper report of 1882 claimed that Turkey red damask table covers made in Scotland or Germany were found in almost every home in every state in the United States.[29] G. W. Harding's catalogue for 1891 also listed 'inexpensive Alhambra quilts for nursery and maidservant use [in] Turkey red, indigo blue or red and blue in combination', costing 2s 11d for the single bed size and 4s 11d for the double bed. Their 'stout Alhambra quilt', again available in Turkey red, cost almost twice as much, while the 'handsome cotton tapestry quilts', at the top end of the market, cost more than half as much again.[30]

Figure 6.6

Glazing the fabric once it had been dyed and printed helped to make it more durable and suitable for a hard-wearing furnishing uses. Unidentified Vale of Leven firm, post-1876.

Cotton; height 506 mm; width 306 mm

National Museums Scotland A.1962.1266.21.1.3460

An insight into the growing emphasis of Turkey red manufacturers' on home furnishings comes from the stands that they mounted at the great exhibitions. At the Manchester exhibition of 1887, for example, William Stirling & Sons' stands were noted for their Turkey red lace curtains and the Turkey red and purple furnishing velvets.[31] The first of the international exhibitions in Glasgow held in 1888 and attracting six million visitors, generated the following lengthy, if waspish, newspaper review of textile displays from arts journalist W. Anderson Smith:

> A very good development in chintz velvets has taken place of recent years, and anything richer or more brilliant could scarcely be desired. The main objection is the lack of novelty in styles. The eye has become so accustomed to the special Turkey red designs that it is apt to confuse the velvet stuffs with the common cotton fabrics, unless there is a marked change in the designs provided. These do not

strike us as sufficiently novel and effective to produce the end desired. The ordinary Turkey red cloth is so soft to the eye in itself that the leap to silken stuffs is not so great as it would be in another colour. The chairs in Wm Stirling & Sons exhibition covered with chintz velvet give a good idea of the effect produced by using this beautiful material. John Orr Ewing & Co. have perhaps the most effectively arranged stands in this class of goods.[32]

The Glasgow International Exhibition of 1888 attracted many notable visitors, including Queen Victoria, who also held a special audience at Blythswood for a select, invited group of industrial exhibitors. One of the invitees was the Manchester firm of F. Steiner & Co. whose Scottish representative was commanded to attend the Queen and her party with a selection of various articles from their Turkey red exhibition stand, 'which she was graciously pleased to examine, and a quantity of the fabrics were commanded to be sent to Balmoral'.[33] F. Steiner & Co., which was a powerful rival to the Scottish firms for many decades, was, in common with the others at the time, facing serious competition for Turkey red sales abroad and was diversifying its products to include other furnishing lines for home sale. As described by W. Anderson Smith at the 1888 Glasgow exhibition, 'this firm is becoming less and less a distinctively Turkey red house and half of their exhibit is given up to very large and effective printings for hangings'.[34]

Though the Turkey red manufacturers sought to develop new printing techniques to reproduce an appearance of higher quality fabric, or even, as in the Steiner case, tapestry hangings, Turkey red cottons remained a product for the mass market. Despite the endeavours of Queen Victoria to offer patronage through purchases for Balmoral, which were almost certainly intended for use in servants' rooms, Turkey red never really penetrated the houses or decorative schemes of the wealthy, who favoured finer and more expensive fabrics with subtle colourings in silk or linen. Turkey red cottons were cheap, cheerful and practical. They were popular and fashionable, but not refined. An article in the *Girl's Own Paper* in 1902, entitled 'How I furnished my bed-sitting-room for twelve pounds', described how to incorporate Turkey red cushion covers and swags with bows on basic furniture to give a warm and comfortable appearance on a tight budget. A mass-circulation magazine like this was aimed at that new and growing phenomenon, the lower-middle class single woman in her teens and early twenties, living, or aspiring to live, on her own in a 'bed-sit' in one of the big cities, while working in an office or departmental store.[35]

Not only popular at home in Britain, cheap Turkey red fabrics were also used for household furnishings throughout the world in places where emigrants from Britain took their domestic habits and culture abroad. The name of the fabric is even celebrated in the title of an American novel, Frances Gilchrist Wood's *Turkey Red: A Novel of the Frontier*, which first appeared in 1919 as a series of short stories in the New York published *The Pictorial Review*. Set in the Dakota frontier territory in the 1880s and drawn from personal experience during the author's own childhood, these sentimental stories recount the struggles of a pioneer community, giving insights into their lives, loves and domestic existence, as in this description of a typical homestead:

> The eight by ten room constituted the entire home. A shed roof slanted from eight feet high on the door and window side to a bit more than five on the other. A bed in one corner took up most of the space, and the remaining necessities were bestowed with the compactness of a ship's cabin. The rough boards of the roof and walls had been hidden by a covering of newspapers, with a row of illustrations pasted picture height. Cushions and curtains of turkey-red calico brightened the homely shack.[36]

Finally, of course, Turkey red fabric was also available locally in the Vale of Leven, for use in household furnishings when the factories sold off their damaged goods and roll ends cheaply to the workers. Richard Holloway, former Bishop of Edinburgh, who was born and raised in the Vale, describes in his autobiography *Leaving Alexandria: A Memoir of Faith and Doubt*, how his father, a dyer in the inter-war years, when the industry was in decline, obtained cloth through less legitimate means:

> My father occasionally stole from his employer, the United Turkey Red, in whose freezing and dilapidated factory on the banks of the River Leven he laboured much of his life away. I say stole, but it did not feel like that to him or to us. It was more like a covert form of redistribution, a way of evening the odds that were heavily stacked against the workers who earned the owners their profits. He would occasionally wrap around his small wiry body the discarded tail-end of a batch of cloth he had been dyeing, and walk through the factory gates at the end of the working day with his raincoat on to disguise his added bulk. Most of it was given away. The contraband would reappear in our neighbour's houses as curtains or cushion covers or cheerful dresses for the women. It helped to brighten our street, with the added spice that it was also an act of subversion.[37]

Quilted garments and quilts

The National Museums Scotland collection of historic clothing includes two items of quilted Turkey red clothing, both manufactured by McLintock & Sons of Barnsley at their Utilitas factory and sold through retail premises such as Misses Fairgrieve's Millinery, Corset and Crinoline Warehouse in Princes Street, Edinburgh. McLintocks, along with rivals Booth & Fox of London, dominated British and Empire supplies of high quality quilts and quilted clothing in the second half of the nineteenth century.

The first item in the Museum's collection is a quilted petticoat, made in the 1870s to a patented design; and the second, more spectacular garment is a woman's full-length dressing gown of about the same period [Fig. 6.7]. Both are printed with small exotic leaves or flowers in bright blues, yellows and greens on a red background, in designs of the type that were developed for the home market. The linings are in plain red. The petticoat has a drawstring waist and the dressing gown is fastened with a bow and hook-and-eye at the neck, and buttons down the front with a belt at the waist. Both garments are fashioned to accommodate the then popular bustle dress-form at the back. The quilted channels are stuffed with eider duck down from Russia and the sewing machine stitching is decorated on the outside with coloured braid. The garments are made of cotton, of either United States or India origin, and probably woven in Lancashire. It is impossible to say if the fabrics were dyed and printed in Scotland or in Lancashire, but the source of manufacture for the garments themselves is indicated through prominent McLintock labels giving patent and design numbers. McLintock's labels later in the century also included details of the prizes they won at international exhibitions. Examples of similar garments by McLintocks or Booth & Fox are in the Bath Fashion Museum, Victoria and Albert Museum, Platt Hall Museum, Manchester and Canon Hall Museum, Barnsley.

McLintock & Sons of Barnsley was founded by James McLintock (1805–

Figure 6.7

Quilted garments like this dressing gown were both practical and comfortable, and when made with Turkey red printed cotton, could also be bright and colourful. Quilted woman's dressing gown with Turkey red dyed and printed cotton. McLintock and Sons, c.1870.

National Museums Scotland

78), son of a Scottish linen weaver, who began his working life as a travelling salesman for a Barnsley linen company, and moved into buying and selling textile remnants on his own account before setting up as a manufacturer of corsets and stays in the 1850s. With his two sons as partners, the firm moved into making quilted undergarments and bedding in the 1860s, for which they registered several patents. They built new prestigious manufacturing premises in Barnsley in 1867 – the Utilitas factory – to accommodate their growing business. An advertisement in the *Birmingham Daily Post*, listing the 'new autumn stock' at Walter Larkin's 'crinoline warehouse' in Bull Street, Birmingham in 1864, declared that they were the 'agents for McLintock's renowned semi cinctorium petticoats, quilts, vests etc'. The same firm, the year before, as well as advertising the 'far-famed' petticoats, referred to sales of the silk down 'toralium' or bed coverlet.[38] McLintocks called their quilts 'toraliums' after the Greek name for bed cover, and they were made in many sizes and coverings, both cotton and satin, and with fillings that ranged from cheap cotton fibre to silk noils and Russian down at the top end. In Edinburgh, departmental store Charles Jenner & Co. of Princes Street, also sold quilted goods, advertising in November 1893 that they were now

> … showing their usual large assortment of best ARCTIC DOWN QUILTS for the WINTER SEASON being mainly the productions of MESSRS BOOTH & FOX and McLINTOCK & SONS.[39]

McLintocks was an ambitious firm with a wide retail distribution, who exhibited their patented designs and goods at international exhibitions, winning a gold medal at the Philadelphia International Exhibition in 1876; bronze at the 1878 Paris Universal Exhibition; and gold again at the 1886 Edinburgh International Exhibition, which was the first of such events to be held in Scotland [Fig. 6.8 and Fig. 6.9]. The company was described in the official catalogue for the Paris exhibition as 'down clothing manufacturers' and 'inventors', and their exhibits in 1878 comprised …

> real Eider and Russian down quilts and skirts. Patent down clothing, silk down toralium quilts and skirts, ladies and gentlemen's dressing gowns and jackets, vests, chest protectors, smoking caps, tea cosies, etc.[40]

For the Edinburgh exhibition, which was opened by Queen Victoria, the firm made a spectacular and costly eiderdown quilt for display on their stand, which was deep red in colour and had the royal coat of

Figure 6.8 (inset)

A label inside a McLintock's Turkey red quilted petticoat of c.1890, advertising the company's success at various international exhibitions. Quilted petticoat, late 19th century.

Private collection

Figure 6.9

This quilted petticoat contains Russian down and the Turkey red printed fabric has a small, multi-coloured floral pattern. Produced by McLintock & Sons of Barnsley, late 19th century.

Private collection

arms and royal monograms embroidered in gold.[41] Spectacle and showmanship was clearly a characteristic of the firm during the life of the founder-owner. At the official opening of the Utilitas works on New Years Eve in 1867, as reported in the press a few days later, to which the workforce and local dignitaries were invited …

> [a] large toralium and semi-cinctorium which has just been completed by Messrs. McLintock and Sons, of Barnsley, was [displayed] with a tea party, concert, and ball.[42]

McLintock quilted garments, such as these in the Museum's collections, were mass-produced for a mainly British middle-class market. They were intimate garments for winter warmth and comfort, signalled in the red colouring. But they were also designed to be seen within a domestic context, with the patterned outer material and decorative braid more expensive than the plainer linings. The Turkey red fabric and the exoticism of the design were intended to signify a hint of luxury as well as sexuality or daring. In contrast, however, and important for the purchasers and wearers of these garment, the written reference within it to the 'purified' down and the official patents created an idea of wholesomeness. Luxury and élite associations were also commonly linked to quilted bed coverings, such as those advertised by Arnott & Co. of Glasgow in the 1880s, which included brand names like the 'New Chatsworth Quilt', which was sold in blue, brown or Turkey red.[43]

The ultimate fate of the 'large toralium and semi-cinctorium' as displayed by McLintocks at their factory opening is nowhere recorded and by the first decades of the twentieth century the fashion for quilted petticoats had passed. The company survived into the twentieth century mainly as manufacturers of down quilts for bedding, though these were mostly made with satin rather than cotton covers, and in muted tasteful pinks and pale blues rather than red. The Utilitas factory finally closed in 1977, over a hundred years after it first opened.

Notes

1. *Glasgow Herald*, 2 August 1889.
2. *Glasgow Herald*, 7 March 1845.
3. See Chapter 2.
4. *Glasgow Herald*, 4 February 1881.
5. T. F. Smith, 'Four aspects of Turkey red: 2', *Quilt Studies*, vol. 1 (1999).
6. *Aberdeen Journal*, 28 December 1853.
7. National Museums Scotland: Turkey Red Collection. Accession no.: A.1962.1266.31.6.
8. *Glasgow Herald*, 6 August 1891.
9. *Glasgow Herald*, 28 June 1886.
10. *Glasgow Herald*, 14 September 1846.
11. *Glasgow Herald*, 3 February 1886.
12. *Glasgow Herald*, 11 April 1894.
13. *Glasgow Herald*, 21 September 1885.
14. *Glasgow Herald*, 5 May 1888; 9 January 1889.
15. Sarah Tytler, *A Houseful of Girls* (London, 1889), p. 121.
16. *Glasgow Herald*, 27 August 1856.
17. *Glasgow Herald*, 1 October 1858.
18. *Glasgow Herald*, 6 September 1859.
19. See Stana Nenadic, 'The social shaping of business behaviour in the nineteenth-century women's garment trades', *Journal of Social History*, 31 (1998), pp. 625–45.
20. *Glasgow Herald*, 5 November 1887.
21. *Glasgow Herald*, 26 May 1900.
22. *Glasgow Herald*, 2 June 1871.
23. *Glasgow Herald*, 24 November 1876.
24. C. Ferguson, *Turkey Red* (York, 2012).
25. See Helen Long, *Victorian Houses and their Details* (Oxford, 2002).
26. *Glasgow Herald*, 31 May 1884.
27. *Glasgow Herald*, 21 August 1888.
28. UGA: UGD13/5/1. Home Sales Book, 1895.
29. *Glasgow Herald*, 21 January 1882.
30. Smith, 'Four aspects of Turkey red: 2.'
31. *Glasgow Herald*, 16 May 1887.
32. *Glasgow Herald*, 24 May 1888.
33. *Glasgow Herald*, 25 August 1888.
34. *Glasgow Herald*, 24 May 1888.
35. *Girl's Own Paper*, 22 Nov, 1902, p. 118. Reproduced in T. Doughty (ed.) *Selections from the Girl's Own Paper, 1880–1907* (London, 2004).
36. Frances Gilchrist Wood, *Turkey Red: A Novel of the Frontier* (New York, 1932) p. 52.
37. Richard Holloway, *Leaving Alexandria: A Memoir of Faith and Doubt* (Edinburgh, 2012), p. 269.
38. *Birmingham Daily Post*, 17 October 1864.
39. *Scotsman*, 20 November 1893.
40. *Official Catalogue of the British Section of the Paris Universal International Exhibition of 1878* (London, 1878).
41. *Cameron's Guide Through the International Exhibition of Industry, Science and Art (and Old Edinburgh), Opened 6 May 1886* (Edinburgh, 1886).
42. *Sheffield & Rotherham Independent*, 2 January 1868.
43. *Glasgow Herald*, 27 April 1881.

Select bibliography

Primary sources

Manuscripts

University of Glasgow Archives (UGA)
Records of the United Turkey Red Co. Ltd.
Manchester County Record Office (MCRO)
United Turkey Red Co. Ltd. (UTR) Minute Books 1–4, 1898–1908.
Mersey Maritime Museum, Liverpool
Jottings from a Sailor's Life. The Journal of Alexander Kidd. Online.

National Archives, Kew (TNA)
Board of Trade Design Registers
National Museums Scotland
Turkey Red Collection
Private Collection
Archibald M. Aitken, 'Recollections of the Turkey red industry.'

Books and journals

'A day at the Barrowfield dyeworks, Glasgow', *The Penny Magazine of the Society for the Diffusion of Useful Knowledge*, 13 (1844), pp. 289–93.

The Continental Monthly: Devoted to Literature and National Policy, August 1864.

David Bremner, *The Industries of Scotland: Their Rise, Progress and Present Condition* (Glasgow, 1869).

Cameron's Guide Through the International Exhibition of Industry, Science and Art (and Old Edinburgh), Opened 6 May 1886 (Edinburgh, 1886).

Henry M. Chester, *Narrative of Expeditions to New Guinea in a Series of Letters* (Brisbane, 1878).

Godey's Lady's Book and Magazine (Philadelphia, 1830–78).

Joseph Irving, *The Book of Dunbartonshire: A History of the County, Burghs, Parishes and Lands, Memoirs of Families, and Notices of Industries Carried on in the Lennox District*, vol. 1 (Edinburgh, 1879).

The Journal of Design and Manufactures (London, 1849–55).

George Macintosh, *Biographical Memoir of the Late Charles Macintosh, FRS of Campsie and Dunchattan* (Glasgow, 1847).

Donald Macleod, *Dumbarton, Vale of Leven and Loch Lomond: Historical, Legendary, Industrial and Descriptive* (Dumbarton, 1884).

Donald Macleod, *Historic Families, Notable People and Memorabilia of the Lennox.* (Dumbarton, 1891).

John Matheson, *England to Delhi: A Narrative of Indian Travel* (London, 1870).

Memoirs and Portraits of One Hundred Glasgow Men (Glasgow, 1886).

Official Catalogue of the British Section of the Paris Universal International Exhibition of 1878 (London, 1878).

Pierre Jacques Papillon, 'Method of dyeing cotton yarn a fixed Turkey red', *The Repertory of Arts, Manufactures and Agriculture*, vol. iv (London, 1804), pp. 105–10.

Report from the Select Committee on Copyright of Designs Together with the Minutes of Evidence Taken Before Them (London 1840).
Textile Manufacturers' Directory of the United States and Canada (New York, 1887).
Robert Tyas, *The Sentiment of Flowers: Or, Language of Flora* (London, 1836).
Sarah Tytler, *A Houseful of Girls* (London, 1889).
Andrew Ure, 'Description of the Great Bandana Gallery in the Turkey red factory of Messrs Monteith and Co. at Glasgow', *The Glasgow Mechanics' Magazine and Annals of Philosophy* (Glasgow, 1831), pp. 7–10.
Alfred Russel Wallace, 'Letter to Joseph Hooke', *The Literary Gazette and Journal of Belles Lettres*. 1854–55. Online.
Who's Who in Glasgow in 1909 (Glasgow, 1909).
Frances Gilchrist Wood, *Turkey Red: A Novel of the Frontier* (New York, 1932).

Newspapers

– Edinburgh Gazette
– Glasgow Herald
– Scotsman
– Supplements to the North British Daily Mail, 1888
– Times of India

Secondary sources

Books and pamphlets

Liz Arthur (ed.), *Seeing Red: Scotland's Exotic Textile Heritage* (Glasgow, 2007).
Sonia Ashmore, *Muslin* (London, 2012).
Barbara Brackman, *Clues in the Calico: A Guide to Identifying and Dating Antique Quilts* (Lafayette, CA, 2009).
Robert Chenciner, *Madder Red: A History of Luxury and Trade, Plant Dyes and Pigments in World Commerce and Art* (Richmond, 2000).
Anthony Cooke, *The Rise and Fall of the Scottish Cotton Industry, 1778–1914* (Manchester, 2010).
Rosemary Crill, *Chintz: Indian Textiles for the West* (London, 2008).
T. Doughty (ed.), *Selections from the Girl's Own Paper, 1880–1907* (London, 2004).
C. Ferguson, *Turkey Red* (York, 2012).
Madeleine Ginsburg, *The Illustrated History of Textiles* (London, 1991).
Amy Butler Greenfield, *A Perfect Red: Empire, Espionage, and the Quest for the Color of Desire* (New York, 2005).
Richard Holloway, *Leaving Alexandria: A Memoir of Faith and Doubt* (Edinburgh, 2012).
Paul Hulton and Lawrence Smith, *Flowers in Art from East and West* (London, 1979).
John Irwin, *The Kashmir Shawl* (London, 1973).
P. Kinchin and J. Kinchin, *Glasgow's Great Exhibitions: 1888, 1901, 1911, 1938, 1988* (Wendlebury, n.d).
Lara Kriegel, *Grand Designs: Labor, Empire and the Museum in Victorian Culture* (London, 2007).
Beverly Lemire, *Fashion's Favourite: The Cotton Trade and the Consumer in Britain, 1660–1800* (Oxford, 1991).
Helen Long, *Victorian Houses and their Details* (Oxford, 2002).
Antonia Lovelace, *Art for Industry: The Glasgow Japan Exchange of 1878* (Glasgow, 1991).
Linda Lynton, *The Sari: Styles, Patterns, History, Techniques* (London, 2002).
John MacKay, *Bleachfields, Printfields and Turkey Red* (Renton, 2011).
Claude Markovits, *Merchants, Traders, Entrepreneurs: Indian Business in the Colonial Era* (Basingstoke, 2008).
Heinz Mode, *The Woman in Indian Art* (Leipzig, 1970).
J. Forbes Munro, *Maritime Enterprise and Empire: Sir William Mackinnon and his Business* (Woodbridge, 2003).
Valerie Reilly, *The Paisley Pattern: The Official Illustrated History* (Glasgow, 1987).
Giorgio Riello and Prasannan Parthasarathi (eds), *The Spinning World: A Global History of Cotton Textiles, 1200–1850* (Oxford, 2011).
Anthony Slaven and Sydney Checkland (eds), *Dictionary of Scottish Business Biography, 1860–1960*, vol.1 (Aberdeen, 1986).
Michael Snodin and John Styles (eds), *Design and the Decorative Arts, Britain 1500–1900* (London, 2001).
John Styles, *The Dress of the People: Everyday Fashion in Eighteenth-Century England* (London, 2007).

Philip Sykas, *The Secret Life of Textiles: Six Pattern Book Archives in North West England* (Bolton, 2005).

Anthony S. Travis, *The Rainbow Makers: The Origins of the Synthetic Dyestuffs Industry in Western Europe* (London, 1993).

C. A. S. Williams, *Chinese Symbolism and Art Motifs: A Comprehensive Handbook on Symbolism in Chinese Art Through the Ages* (Vermont, 2006).

Articles and essays

Sonia Ashmore, 'Owen Jones and the V&A Collections', *V&A Online Journal*, 1 (2008).

Stanley Chapman, 'The commercial sector', in Mary B. Rose (ed.) *The Lancashire Cotton Industry: A History Since 1700* (Preston, 1996), pp. 63–93.

S. D. Chapman, 'Quantity versus quality in the British industrial revolution: the case of printed textiles', *Northern History*, 21 (1985), pp. 175–92.

S. Cheang, 'Dragons in the drawing room: Chinese embroideries in British homes, 1860–1949', *Textile History*, 24:2 (2008), pp. 223–49.

F. Driver and S. Ashmore, 'The mobile museum: Collecting and circulating Indian textiles in Victorian Britain', *Victorian Studies* 52:3 (2010), pp. 353–84.

Alexander Engel, 'Colouring markets: The industrial transformation of the dyestuff business revisited', *Business History*, 54:1 (2012), pp. 10–29.

David Greysmith, 'Patterns, piracy and protection in the textile printing industry', *Textile History*, 14:2 (1983), pp. 165–94.

D. M. Higgins and Geoffrey Tweedale, 'The trade mark question and the Lancashire cotton textile industry', *Textile History*, 27:2 (1996), pp. 207–28.

Francina Irwin, 'Scottish eighteenth-century chintz and its design', part I and II, *The Burlington Magazine*, vol. 107, no. 750 and 751 (1965), pp. 452–58, 510–15.

E. Kramer, 'Master or market? The Anglo-Japanese textile designs of Christopher Dresser', *Journal of Design History*, 19.3 (2006), pp. 197–214.

Ada K. Longfield, 'William Kilburn and the earliest copyright acts for cotton printing designs', *The Burlington Magazine*, 95:604 (1953), pp. 230–33.

Agnes M. M. Lyons, 'The textile fabrics of India and Huddersfield cloth industry', *Textile History*, 27:2 (1996), pp. 172–94.

Stana Nenadic, 'Exhibiting India in nineteenth century Scotland and the impact on commerce, industry and design', *Journal of Scottish Historical Studies* (2013 forthcoming).

Stana Nenadic, 'Industrialisation and the Scottish people', in T. M. Devine and J. Wormald (eds) *The Oxford Handbook of Modern Scottish History* (Oxford, 2012), pp. 405–22.

Stana Nenadic, 'The social shaping of business behaviour in the nineteenth-century women's garment trades', *Journal of Social History*, 31 (1998), pp. 625–45.

R. A. Peel, 'Alizarin users defy a threat', *The Dyer and Textile Printer* (June, 1956), pp. 1013–14.

R. A. Peel, 'Perkin and the Scottish alizarin dyers', *The Dyer and Textile Printer* (May, 1956), pp. 851–54.

R. A. Peel, 'Zenith of alizarin prints: Impact of new ideas and dyes on the old craftmanship', *The Dyer and Textile Printer* (July, 1956), p.119–20.

T. F. Smith, 'Four aspects of Turkey red: 2', *Quilt Studies*, vol. 1 (1999).

Naomi Tarrant, 'The Turkey red dyeing industry in the Vale of Leven', in J. Butt and K. Ponting (eds), *Scottish Textile History* (Aberdeen, 1987), pp. 37–47.

Anthony S. Travis, 'Between broken root and artificial alizarin: Textile arts and manufacturers of madder', *History and Technology: An International Journal*, 12:1 (1994), pp. 1–22.

Sally Tuckett and Stana Nenadic, 'Colouring the Nation: A new in-depth study of the Turkey red pattern books in the National Museums of Scotland', *Textile History*, 42:2 (2012), pp. 140–51.

Anthony Webster, 'The strategies and limits of gentlemanly capitalism: the London East India agency houses, provincial commercial interests, and the evolution of British economic policy in South and South East Asia, 1800–50,' *Economic History Review*, 59.4 (2006), pp. 743–64.

Rudold Wittkower, 'Eagle and serpent: a study in the migration of symbols', *Journal of the Warburg Institute*, 2:4 (1939), pp. 293–325.

Select index of names and organisations

A

Albert Coates & Co., London, (shipping agents) 116
Alexander, Robert 9
Alexandria Works, Vale of Leven 10, 14, 15
Allan, David 74
American Civil War 99, 105, 111
American Singer Sewing Machine Company 129
Anderson Smith, W. 133–34
Anderson, Wright & Co. 20
Archibald Orr Ewing & Co. 1, 7, 10, 11–13, 20, 29, 36, 39, 45, 52, 53, 55, 58, 59, 63, 87–88, 117, 119
Arnott & Co., Glasgow (store) 139

B

Bannerman's, Edinburgh (remnant warehouse) 123
Barr, James 11
Barrowfield printworks, Glasgow 28, 97
Bath Fashion Museum 136
Beard, Daniel C. 99
Bell, Thomas 33
Bethnal Green Museum of Childhood, London 125
Board of Trade, London 53, 56, 100
Board of Trustees for Fisheries and Manufactures 3, 26
Bombay Pattern Book 7, 20, 39, 43, 49, 50, 52–53, 76, 105, 106
Booth & Fox, London 123–24, 136, 137
Bowman, Madam (dressmaker) 129
Bremner, David 27, 34, 36
British Alizarine Company Ltd 39
British Sewing Machine Company 129
Buchanan, John 47–48, 69

C

Calico Printers Association, Manchester 14–15, 16–17
Canon Hall Museum, Barnsley 136
Charles Jenner & Co., Edinburgh (store) 137
Christie, John F. 36
Christie Jnr, John 10, 14, 15, 39, 61
Christie, John Hyde 10, 15, 20, 38, 39
Clyde Print Works and Bleachery, Rhode Island, USA 103
Cole, Henry 51, 67
Colouring the Nation 2
Copland & Lye, Glasgow (drapers) 125, 127, 130, 132
Cordale Printworks, Vale of Leven 4, 5, 14–15, 123
County Clerk of Dunbartonshire 29
Croftengea Works, Vale of Leven 9, 11

D

D. J. Macdonald & Co. 62
Dale, David 3
Dalquhurn Dyeworks, Vale of Leven 4–5, 39
Defoe, Daniel 2
Design Act of 1839 51, 52
Design Act of 1842 51, 53
Dillichip works, Vale of Leven 11
Docharty, James 46–47
Doulton & Co., London 62
Dresser, Christopher 79

E

E. & J. Steegmann 58
East India Company 2, 104, 106, 107
European and Australian Royal Mail Company 119
Ewart, Latham & Co., Bombay 43
Ewing, Archibald Orr 11, 12–13
Ewing, John Orr 9, 11, 12, 20
Exhibitions 44, 58–64
 – Crystal Palace (1851) 7–8, 58, 59–60, 82, 128
 – Edinburgh (1886) 58, 137
 – Glasgow (1846) 60–61
 – Glasgow (1888) 58, 62–64, 133–34
 – Glasgow (1901) 15, 58, 62, 64
 – Glasgow, (1911) 58
 – London India and Colonial (1886) 62
 – Manchester (1856) 58
 – Manchester (1887) 62, 133

145

– Paris (1855) 80
– Paris (1867) 38, 61, 67
– Paris (1878) 61, 137
– Philadelphia (1876) 137

F

Factory Acts 29
– Commission 29
Farrow & Ball 23
Fereneze Print Works, Barrhead 103
Forrester & Co., Shanghai, China 110
Frederick Steiner & Co., Germany and Lancashire/Manchester 7, 10, 63, 109, 116, 135

G

G. W. Harding, York (linen warehouse) 133
Glasgow Art Club 44
Glasgow Chamber of Commerce 13
Glasgow (Government) School of Design 47, 48–49
Gordon, Trokes, Leitch & Co., New York, USA 98
Grey & Co., Bombay (commission agents) 125

H

Henry Monteith & Co. 27–28, 35, 46, 47, 58, 59, 61–62, 97, 99, 119, 128
Henry Murty, Arbroath (draper) 133
Herman Lucius & Co. 43
Hodgshon Sumner & Co., Montreal, Canada 103
Holloway, Richard (former Bishop of Edinburgh) 135
Hood, William 116
Huschke & Co., Switzerland 105

I

Inglis & Wakefield, Manchester & Busby 44

J

James Findlay & Co., Glasgow 62, 109
James Thomson & Co., Lancashire 51, 53
Jardine Matheson, China (transport company) 113
John Black & Co. 61–62
John M. Campbell & Sons, Glasgow (ship owners) 112
John Orr Ewing & Co. 1, 2, 7, 9–11, 12, 13, 14, 19, 20, 26, 29, 34, 35, 36, 38, 39, 50, 52–53, 55, 56, 58, 60, 61, 62, 63, 69, 82, 84, 85, 87, 89, 100, 109, 110–11, 112, 113, 115, 119
John Ross & Co., Melbourne, Australia (textile firm) 120
John Todd & Co. 9, 11, 20
Jones, Owen 67
Joseph Peel & Co. 51
Journal of Design and Manufacture 48, 51, 67

K

Kelly & Co. 7
Kelvingrove Art Gallery and Museum 58
Koechlin, Daniel 28

L

Levenbank Works 11
Levenbank Printfield 11
Levenfield Printworks 2, 9
Levine, Madam(e) (dressmaker) 129
Liberty & Co. 74
Lindsay, James 44
Livingstone, Dr David 119, 124

M

Macintosh, George 28
Mackinnon, William 106
Manchester County Record Office 17
Manchester Design School 51

Marshall & Snelgrove, London (store) 133
Matheson, John 5, 6–7, 31–32, 56, 106–8
McEwan, Tom 44
McGonagall, William 87
McGregor, General Sir Duncan 85
McLeod, John, Tasmania, Australia (retailer) 119
McLintock & Sons, Barnsley 124, 136–37, 138, 139
McLintock, James 136–37
McManus Museum and Gallery, Dundee 130–131
Messrs Lewes & Co., Shettleston (abattior) 26
Misses Fairgrieve's Millinery, Corset and Crinoline Warehouse, Edinburgh 123–24, 136
Morris, William 71, 74, 131
Muir, Brown & Co. 103
Muir, John 62, 109

N

National Archives, Kew 51–52
National Museums Scotland Turkey Red Collection 7, 16–20, 25, 30, 32, 35, 36, 37, 39, 43, 44, 49, 68, 69, 72, 74, 75, 79, 82, 85, 87, 89, 92, 105, 110–11, 114, 116, 127–28, 131
New Lanark 3

P

Papillon, Pierre Jacques 26, 27, 28
Perkin, William Henry 38
Pettigrew & Stephens, Glasgow (store) 130
Philadelphia Museum of Art 88
Philip & Kennedy of Union Buildings, Aberdeen (drapers) 125
Platt Hall Museum, Manchester 124, 136

Pollockshaws Printfield Company 2
Pullars of Perth 38

Q

Quilters' Guild, York 130

R

R. Alexander & Co. 9, 10, 20, 84
Reoch, Robert 103
Rowan, McNab & Co., Sydney, Australia (retailer) 119
Royal Institution, Edinburgh 60
Royal Polytechnic Warehouse sale, 1871 130

S

Scotts & Co., Greenock (shipbuilders) 112
Select Committee on Copyright of Designs 56–57
Shanghai Pattern Book 20, 110–11, 112–13
Simpson, Maule & Nicholson, London and Edinburgh 6
Social Science Association and British Association 7
Society of Arts, London 25
Society of Dyers and Colourists, Bradford 17
Steiner, Frederick 10, 28
Stevenson & Mckenzie 58
Stirling, William 4
Stobart Sons & Co., Manitoba, Canada 103

T

Textile Manufacturers' Directory of the United States and Canada 102
Thomas Watkins, Hamilton, Canada 103
Thomson, James 51
Todd & Higginbotham 44
Todd, Shortridge & Co. 2

U

United Turkey Red Company Ltd 1, 13–16, 20, 29–30, 32, 36, 39, 40, 64, 84–85, 109, 113, 114, 116
University of Glasgow 51, 103
– Archives 16
– Scottish Business Archives 17
Utilitas factory, Barnsley 136, 137, 138, 139

V

Victoria and Albert Museum 136
Victoria, Queen 38, 60, 82, 83, 87, 100, 127, 134, 137

W

Wallace, Alfred Russel 110, 113–14
Walter Larkin's, Birmingham (crinoline warehouse) 137
Watson, John Forbes 48, 92
Weldon's Home Dressmaker 129
West Dunbartonshire Council 44
William Leckie, New York, USA
William Stirling & Sons 1, 2–3, 4–8, 9, 13, 19, 20, 25–26, 27, 29, 31, 34, 36, 43, 48, 49, 52–53, 55, 56, 59, 62, 72, 75–76, 82, 89, 99, 103, 105, 106, 110, 123, 128, 133
Wilson, Misses (dressmaker) 129
Wood, Frances Gilchrist 135
Wylie & Lochhead, Glasgow (store) 133
Wylie, John 10, 11

Y

Young, Mrs (dressmaker) 129
Yule & Co., Calcutta, India 110